Human Behavior and the Helping Professions

About the book. . .

This book stresses the universals of the human experience in helping and in being helped and offers a panorama of various methods of helping which ranges from behavior modification to psychotherapy, from helping in one-to-one relationships to group and family therapy. It emphasizes the importance of a congruence between personality and career choice as well as that of a congruence between personality and methodology practiced within the profession chosen. It suggests ways of overcoming difficulties in relationships between helper and client or patient based on differences in age, sex, race, and historical destiny reflected in loyalties to one's own background and highlighting moral problems which practitioners of medicine and social work have to solve as a result of technological and social change. Attention is paid to problems for clients, patients, and professionals who have to give and receive help under the constraints of beaurocratic organization.

The book is the result of the author's work as liaison person among practitioners of sociology, psychiatry, and social work. It is based on problems identified and material presented in numerous seminars, institutes, and lectures for psychiatric residents, practicing social workers in continuing education courses, nurses, lectures to first- and second-year medical students, and a seminar for graduate and undergraduate students in the sociology of health and welfare. It attempts to fill the gap created by the neglect of historical and philosophical perspectives in the literature on helping methodologies.

Human Behavior and the Helping Professions

Otto Pollak, Ph.D.
The Wharton School
The University of Pennsylvania
Philadelphia, Pennsylvania

S P Books Division of
SPECTRUM PUBLICATIONS, INC.
New York

Distributed by Halsted Press
A Division of John Wiley & Sons

New York   Toronto   London   Sydney

SPECTRUM PUBLICATIONS, INC.
86-19 Sancho Street, Holliswood, N.Y. 11423

Distributed solely by the Halsted Press division of John Wiley & Sons, Inc., New York

Library of Congress Cataloging in Publication Data

Pollak, Otto, 1908-
   Human behavior and the helping professions.

   1. Social service. 2. Human behavior. 3. Psychotherapy. I. Title. [DNLM: 1. Behavior. 2. Psychotherapy. WM420 P771h]
HV41.P64   360   76-2576
ISBN 0-470-15041-6

This book,
like all my books,
is dedicated to Trudie

About the author. . .

Otto Pollak received his J.D. degree from the
University of Vienna in 1930, his M.A. in 1940
and M.S.W. in 1941 from Bryn Mawr College,
and his Ph.D. in 1947 from The University of
Pennsylvania. He has taught Sociology at The
University of Pennsylvania since 1942, and is
presently Visiting Professor in the Departments
of Psychiatry at both the Medical College of
Pennsylvania and the Thomas Jefferson Medical
College, both since 1973. Since 1962, he has
been Director of the Graduate Training Program in the Sociology of Health and Welfare
at The University of Pennsylvania. He has been
Principal Investigator in the Administration on
Aging's Utilization Study of a Senior Center
(1967-1971) and was Director of Research at
the Sidney Hillman Medical Center (1966-
1971).

CONTENTS

ACKNOWLEDGMENTS

This book is the result of many professional and personal experiences which go back over many years. Among the persons who contributed to them, I should like to mention first my late father, Dr. Jacob Pollak, a general practitioner in Vienna. In the days between the two World Wars, a physician's office in Vienna was attached to his home and a youngster could not help living on the fringes the work of a physician who was his father.

Being married to Dr. Gertrude K. Pollak, a social worker who was a liberated woman long beofre the term was coined, has given me decades of conversations about the helping process from which I have benefited greatly. This book is dedicated to her as a token of my gratitude.

The experience of being helped I owe to my analyst, Dr. Kenneth E. Appel. The philosophy and historical perspective expressed in this book I owe in great part to the privilege of having had many conversations with my late friend, Dr. Robert Waelder.

Many productive professional associations have contributed as well—foremost among them my long time association as collaborator and friend with Dr. Maurice R. Friend, child psychoanalyst in New York, and with three eminent psychiatrists, Dr. Morris Brody, Dr. Edward Gottheil, and Dr. Laurence H. Snow.

A great input came from many psychiatric residents at the Hospital of the University of Pennsylvania, Thomas Jefferson Medical College, and the Medical College of Pennsylvania, who attended seminars which I have conducted over the last fifteen years.

Too numerous to mention are the social workers who, as members of institutes and of the summer school sessions at the School of Social Work of Tulane university and as colleagues at the Jewish Board of Guardians, have enriched my observations and reflections on the work of the helping professions.

A special note of gratitude is due to my graduate students in Sociology and from the field of Nursing in which it was my privilege to teach.

It has also been my good fortune to have as a secretary Mrs. Florence M. Dougherty, who has been a patient friend and a never failing helper in coping with the many chores which writing a book inflicts upon the author and his associates.

Otto Pollak

Human Behavior and the Helping Professions

CHAPTER I

HELPING IN HISTORICAL PERSPECTIVE

While professional helping for people in distress is a relative new-comer to western civilization, helping as such is part of the Judeo-Christian tradition and dates back to at least Biblical times. Recently, however, the nature of distress which helping requires has undergone considerable change. In Biblical times, in the Middle Ages, and up to the middle of the nineteenth century, distress was largely defined as economic want. Distress was equivalent to being poor, and it was deemed a religious and moral obligation of the rich to divert part of their bounty to the less fortunate. A tithe, one-tenth of the crop, was to be left unharvested by the land owner for the poor. Jewish tradition in the Middle Ages and up until the disappearance of the *shtetl* culture in Russia prescribed that rich men on holidays should invite poor people to their dinner tables. In medieval Christianity, monasteries provided soup for the poor. Under the Eliza-bethan Poor Law, England started to provide indoor relief in special institutions called "poor houses."

The religious and moral obligation behind these various types of giving and even more the compliance with it was probably based on the experience of anxiety of the rich that their wealth was either illgotten or in jeopardy because a more powerful person might covet it. To be wealthy in an ocean of poverty must have seemed to be a provocation of destiny—up until recent times poverty was universal and wealth the exception.

Wealth is usually associated with power and, in the experience of man, corrupts. To the powerful, diverting a part of their wealth to the powerless would, therefore, be experienced as atonement—the cathedrals of Europe testify to the need of the powerful to gain forgiveness for the corruption they sensed in themselves as a result of their good fortune.

In a famous poem Friedrich von Schiller has expressed man's apprehension about good fortune which cannot be redeemed by sacrifice. It tells of a Greek king who was successful in all his undertakings, rich in territory and treasure and who, to propitiate the gods, pulled a valuable ring from his finger and threw it into the sea. Relieved, he sat down to dinner a few hours afterwards, was served a freshly caught fish and, on cutting into it, found his ring. Frightened at his inability to appease the gods, people fled from his court. In modern times Albert Camus has given a secular version of the discomfort of the fortunate by saying that it may be shameful to be happy by oneself.[1] In recent times distress has been redefined in large measure with the widespread redistribution of wealth. This is due in part to the vast increase of industrialized production of material goods, partly due to the power of union organizations, and partly due to the transfer of the function of relieving material want from private individuals and industry to big government. The most important factor in redefining distress, however, has resulted from the ascendency of psychiatry. In the late nineteenth and early twentieth centuries, distress has been redefined to encompass intrapersonal and interpersonal discomfort. People are entitled to relief not only from poverty but also from psychiatric discomforts. While material want seems to be the problem of a minority, psychiatric distress is recognized as universal and legitimated as a condition requiring help. With this shift, however, there occurred a strange change in the perception of the helper. Giving material relief to people who did not have food or money, or sufficient clothing and shelter did not seem to require any training or experience. With the legitimization of psychiatric types of distress which demand help, the will to help was soon recognized as inefficient and the helpers needed training to give the proper help. This occurred first in medicine when the specialization of psychiatry was established. Very soon it spread to social work and is now being recognized through the training of paraprofessionals who work in community mental health centers. Helping therefore occurs in a framework in which both material and psychiatric want are considered objects of helping and where the helper must be trained for his job. Actually modern data-processing capabilities, modern forms of banking and modern forms of legal service and inquiry tend to separate the helping task from the giving of material relief and to confine it to other sources of distress. This has found expression in public welfare where the establishment of eligibility is separated from service and the personnel in charge of service identified as staff requiring special training.

A third determinant of helping as it is practiced today and needed today is the increased secularization which deprives people of any hope of compensatory reward in an afterlife, a hope which formerly sustained people in distress. The famous saying of Jesus that it would be easier for a camel to pass through the needle's eye than for a rich man to attain heaven provided, of course, comfort to the disadvantaged who had to cope with the inequity of privilege. Further, it gave life the sustaining aspect of infinity which made it easier for the poor and the distressed to tolerate their immediate condition and look instead to an infinity which promised better things to come. It was also an expectation not subject to reality testing and, therefore, a belief not subject to disappointment in the present. With the increasing loss of a belief in God and a life after death, the distress of the current experience could not be minimized and seemed to require relief in the here and now, if relief was to come at all.

In this orientation the philosophy of existentialism has become essential for an understanding of our practice of professional helping and seems to require an early place in any treatise devoted to a survey and analysis of helping in modern times. The philosophy of existentialism has unfortunately been developed by German philosophers who write in a tradition of cumbersome and often almost unintelligible expression. The temptation to explore rather than elucidate may have been a reaction to the classic lucidity, particularly that of Aristotle. To represent to English-speaking audiences the thought content of German philosophy is, therefore, a very difficult task. It is doubly difficult because the representative philosopher of existentialism, Martin Heidegger,[2] has written a linguistic philosophy in which the thought content is developed from the meaning of German words such as *dasein, Geworfenheit, Befindlichkeit, vorhanden* and *zuhanden.* To an English-speaking person for whom these words require translation, the nature of Heidegger's thinking cannot be conveyed with the same convincing power with which it comes to a person born into the German language. Existentialism suffers not only in direct translation but also through the writings of Jean Paul Sartre, who had to pierce the fog of German philosophical expression and present the underlying ideas with the clarity of the French idiom. Moreover, he elaborated them and gave them implications which Heidegger may not have intended. When his works, in turn were translated into the noncommital English language, both original German texts and translations of Sartre lost the redeeming feature of thought completion which characterizes German and French.[3] In spite of these difficulties, existentialism provides Americans with some means of problem finding and some attempts to problem solution.

Heidegger starts with the original and permanent question of philosophy: What is it that can be known? To Aristotle the answer was simple—things and people who are accessible to the person seeking knowledge. To Heidegger the object of knowledge is not only what is, but what can be. The object of knowledge is transferred from actual reality to potential reality. Things that exist are, therefore, only concretizations of potentials that might also lead to other concretizations. This has gone deep into the searching and thinking of middle-class young people. It represents the exploration of the Women's Movement, of people who experiment with alternate forms of marriage, of the mental health movement, of the permanent search of adolescents to find themselves. For people in all these movements, it is important to consider possibilities of transference from their present reality into other realities or existences. In other words, people are dissatisfied with their concretizations and look for an expression of other potential concretizations. In that sense the concept of finding oneself is erroneous. People who try to find themselves have found themselves but are dissatisfied with their findings. It is natural that people so dissatisfied would be looking for help in their efforts to change the concreteness of their being into another concreteness.

This search for another existence is limited by two phenomena which also find their elucidation in existential philosophy and conceptualization. One is the phenomenon of being born into a biological destiny such as sex and race and being forced to live out a certain period of history, of being born into a certain socioeconomic status which determines a type of socialization and exposure to a set of inhibitions which vary from group to group. Man has the ability to evaluate the result of his being born into such a set of determinants and frequently comes out with a negative evaluation. Frequently he spends his life protesting against these determinants and looking for ways of changing their results. The helping professions are frequently seen as allies in these protests or at least as listeners to the protest, thus permitting the catharsis of the expression of discontent.

The search for another existence is usually expressed as a search for authenticity in living. People feel that the results of their being born into life results in the compulsion to be like others whereas they would really like to be different. They find that they do not express the most desirable potential of their being but are forced into a concretization which seems to be desirable to their parents, spouses, employers, or groups in society who are more powerful than they. These protests are experienced as struggles in which auxiliaries are needed. Our civilization provides these auxiliaries in the form of trained helpers, such as psychiatrists and social workers, or people who have won a measure of liberation from the same compulsions, such as Alcoholics Anonymous and Synanon.

Another concept of existential philosophy adds an element of urgency to these efforts and demands for being helped. Man's awareness of his mortality, which he experiences in advance as a dread of nothingness, makes the experience of living one of running towards one's own death. From this awareness of limitation of time comes concern about the results of living in view of these limitations in time as well as in circumstances. This results in the experience of worrying (*Sorge*) which English scholars have translated into "care." This is not a literal translation—it is an elaboration of Heidegger thought. He who worries cares. To alleviate the worry, this care is usually extended to others whom one loves, i.e., for whom one cares, and to self for whom one frequently cares either too much or too little. It seems to be common to say that people who want help care too much for themselves and too little for others, and that people who give help are sometimes driven to care too much for others and too little for themselves.

Since all these efforts to change existence must be carried out under the limitation of natural life and impending death, the problem of temporality becomes one of the key issues in helping. It is perhaps significant that psychoanalysis flourished at a time when the awareness of temporality was not as pronounced as it has become in the 1950's and 1960's under the threat of atomic annihilation. Drug therapies, the wide acclaim of behavior modification and, ultimately, the transfer from clinical to social intervention—all express a sense of urgency which can be understood only from the angle of temporality which has entered the awareness of modern man.

One of man's greatest threats and actual discomforts is loneliness. This is a psychological result of biological destiny. The human being is born helpless and for extended periods of time requires the service of another human being, usually adult and "caring" for him. In the past this was usually a female who provided permanence of care in the life of the infant and child. Persons and the constancy of the caring person therefore, have become pervasive need-satisfiers of the human condition and, in the preindustrial past have been easily provided by members of the family—persons whose availability and constancy have been destroyed through the demands of industrialization. First, they have taken the father out of the home, then they have taken brothers and sisters out of the home and, frequently, out of the community, and have put distance between members of kinship. The entrance of women into the labor market and the increasing participation of women in the professions have separated spouses not only in time but frequently in geographical space. Under such conditions many human beings experience loneliness to an unprecedented degree and therefore must buy company, care and constancy in the professional marketplace. If one has an appointment with a psychiatrist, a social worker or a community mental health worker, one has secured for himself a person of predictable nature who will provide predictable care for a predictable period of time. From this point of view, helping becomes first and foremost a process rather than a production. It is the misfortune of the helping professions that their work is viewed as a production that is evaluated according to the technical industrial model—a production which provides measurable results. One is supposed to get into it in distress and come out of it not only free of the old distress but also fortified against new distress. When people reenter analysis, go back for more help to a social worker, or shift from one social movement to another, there is always the suspicion that the earlier form of help has been ineffective. This completely misunderstands and disregards the nature of the helping process and the nature of the person who re-- quires help.

Human beings are open systems who maintain themselves in permanent exchanges. They are systems and form systems. Two systems represented by spouses form a marital system. When children result, the marital system creates parent-child systems and, if there are at least two children, they create a sibling system. Through the participation of the spouses in the labor market, they may both enter organization systems and school-age children bring the familial system into interaction with the educational system. Health care brings the family into repeated contact with the medical system. The list of system connections to which the human existence must respond could easily be prolonged.

Since it is the nature of a system that change in one part will produce change in all parts, helping usually produces side effects not originally visualized by either the helper or the person who seeks help. A person during psychoanalysis may find that his marital partner becomes disturbed. Parents seek help for their children and find that their marriage is affected. A schizophrenic youngster is hospitalized and his brother who formerly was well begins to show psychotic systems. These developments were first identified in the 1940's by Mildred Burgum[4] and Bela Mittelmann[5] and have led to the development of family therapy and ultimately, through the work of Ross Speck, to network therapy.

Helping is therefore likely to proceed from utopian expectations to non-utopian results, reminding us of Freud's famous dictum that the outcome of a successful psychoanalysis is the replacement of neurotic misery by common everyday misery. It is difficult for people in our society to accept the unavoidability of side effects of medication. As a result, helpers are likely to oversell and people who need help to overbuy the results of available methods of help.

This requires a scrutiny of the nature and meaning of change. It is the experience of maturity that every change has its own price and that there are no bargains. People who suffer from childlessness and finally manage to get children find that children demand care and attention which take away the care and attention spouses have formerly given to one another. They find out that children hardly ever grow up the way the parents desire. People who have been striving for higher income find that, with the achievement of the higher income, their expenses go up. People who manage to seed a lawn successfully find that the lawn has to be cut. People who fight sleeplessness with medication at night find themselves drowsy in the morning—the list goes on and on.

Therefore, what helping can provide is not freedom from discomfort; rather, it can provide change of discomforts. This is not cynicism but an affirmation of man's need for a dialogue with destiny, of his liberation from the monotony and doom of being saddled by the same discomfort. Washington Irving[6] and more recently Ivan Boszormenyi-Nagy[7] have pointed out that the essence of life is change, not the attainment of bliss. What helping can do therefore is to affirm and stimulate man's powers of change.

By helping a person to change one may not be able to help him to remove a discomfort and remain otherwise the same person but one may have helped to cure the disease of hope which results from the feeling of helplessness in adversity. In that sense it can be seen that helping is man's ally in his struggle with helplessness.

REFERENCES

1. Albert Camus, *The Plague*, New York, Vintage Books, 1972, p. 194.
2. Martin Heidegger, *Existence and Being*, Chicago, W. Regnery Co., 1949; *Being and Time*, New York, Harper & Row, 1962.
3. Jean Paul Sartre, *Existential Psychoanalysis*, New York, Philosophical Library, 1953; *Being and Nothingness*, New York Philosophical Library, 1956.
4. Mildred Burgum, "The Father Gets Worse: A Child Guidance Problem," *American Journal of Orthopsychiatry*, XII (July 1942) p. 474.
5. Bela Mittelmann, "Complementary Neurotic Reaction in Intimate Relationships," *Psychoanalytic Quarterly*, Vol. 13 October 1944, pp. 482-483
6. Washington Irving, *Tales of a Traveller*, New York & London, G. P. Putnam's Sons, 1897, pp. 5-6.
7. Ivan Boszormenyi-Nagy, "The Concept of Change in Conjoint Family Therapy" in *Psychotherapy for the Whole Family*, Alfred S. Friedman, *et al.*, New York, Springer Publishing Co., 1965, pp. 305-317.

CHAPTER II

BASIC HUMAN NEEDS AND LEARNING OF NEED FULFILLMENT

In the last chapter we have proposed that enabling a person to bring about change in his condition is the essence of helping. This implies that people who do not require help bring about change by themselves and that change is the essence of human behavior. It seems appropriate, therefore, to represent the elements of human behavior as the theoretical underpinning of helping behavior and to establish thereby its relatedness to human behavior in general.

The following presentation is based on three axioms:

1. All human beings are open systems who maintain themselves through exchanges.
2. Human behavior is wish relevant (has purpose).
3. Most human behavior is learned, i.e., based on past experience—behavior which has resulted in satisfactory outcome is likely to be repeated, behavior that has brought pain is likely to be extinguished.[1]

The first axiom suggests that human beings have boundaries but also openings in these boundaries which serve input and output. The life-maintaining functions of the use of these openings in the system come easily to acceptance when we visualize their dysfunction. A person who cannot chew, such as a toothless old man, suggests powerlessness—a reduction of his intake to liquids corresponds to helplessness of the infant in the first few months of life. A person who cannot eliminate waste products will toxify his body within a relatively short period of time and will require surgical relief. The most elaborate use of communication occurs through language which requires openings of the mouth and the ear drums for operation. Human beings frequently precede kissing or intercourse with a meeting of eyes as if signals pouring forth from the eyes of one were received by the other. Compared with the rich repertoire of verbal language, body language seems to be primitive indeed. Working largely within the boundaries of the human body represented by the skin, it can essentially express only approach and withdrawal, care and hostility through establishing closeness or distance and through posturing (turning toward and turning away). It is, however, less frequently in the range of awareness of the person who exhibits it, and is therefore less likely to be used for lying and sometimes outside of the range of lying, as in impotence and frigidity. The likelihood of truthfulness in body language is also supported by a significant observation made by the Palo Alto Group of Psychiatry in the identification of the double bind.[2] This is a condition where verbal language and body language of a mother give contradictory signals to a child, possibly leading to the confusion and withdrawal of the schizophrenic.

It is a common experience that before action, a human being visualizes a desired result. He visualizes the future and undertakes to bring it about. People whose purposes cannot be understood appear to us enigmatic, dangerous and frequently disturbed. Human beings try to understand one another by believing to understand their purposes. Human behavior is therefore presumed to be wish relevant. It is one of the fascinations of psychiatry to seek out purpose behind apparent purposelessness. To make sense out of nonsense seems to me a basic human need, namely, to establish one's similarity with others by ascribing to them purpose because we experience purpose ourselves. The assumption of purpose as an element of human behavior thus expresses a need for community with others.

It is one of the disturbing discoveries of psychoanalysis that there is reason to believe that under certain circumstances, human beings do not know their own purpose although they believe that they do. The phenomenon of rationalization suggesting that people who believe they have good reasons, i.e., purpose, to account for their behavior, might on the basis of other information, demonstrate to others that they pursue other purposes. This is one of the disturbances in effective human behavior and interaction. A dramatic demonstration of this phenomenon was the famous umbrella experiment which Charcot had used effectively until it misfired in the presence of Freud. In simple terms, the umbrella experiment was designed to convince people of the effectiveness of posthypnotic orders. To refute the proposition of spontaneous recovery, Charcot, who had treated disturbed patients with posthypnotic orders in which he commanded them to drop their symptoms, devised a posthypnotic order which, if effective, could not be explained by spontaneity. He put patients in a trance and commanded them at a specific hour on the day of their next visit, to take an umbrella from the stand in their hallway, carry it into their living room, open it, close it, and put it back. Patients always reported that they had done so when asked by the professor about a detailed report of their day and always, when asked, were unable to explain this apparently bizarre behavior. One day, however, one patient gave a perfectly rational explanation—he said that rain had been threatening, that he had seemed to remember that there was a hole in his umbrella which he had asked his wife to mend and could not ask her because she was not in, and that he wanted to make sure before leaving that the hole was mended. Since there was not sufficient light in the hallway, he had to take the umbrella into the living room where light was better. Having found no hole in the umbrella, he had put it back. The hostility of Charcot's opponents seemed to have a field day. Only to the scientifically trained genius of Sigmund Freud, the effectiveness of the posthypnotic order seemed to be unchallenged by this explanation. The element of the time specified in the order and observed by the patient was not accounted for by his explanation, and Freud had the first inkling that people may have perfectly acceptable reasons for what they do, believe that these are the real reasons of their behavior, while we may have other sources of information suggesting other reasons. He had come across the phenomenon of rationalization.[3]

The assumption of purpose as a universal element of human behavior is, of course, not refuted by the phenomenon of rationalization but suggests to us a risk in the acceptance of professed purpose as an explanation of human behavior. If people under certain circumstances may not know the real reasons for their behavior, they cannot be counted upon to state their purposes correctly, even if they think they do.

While the first two propositions have been presented as universal, the third one cannot be presented with such a claim. It is true that in the course of development much human behavior is learned, that it is a repetition of past behavior which has been found to be effective or avoidance of behavior which has brought pain, but this presupposes the repetition of the situation. Since human beings go through different developmental stages, and since the conditions under which they have to apply learning change over periods of time—sometimes with startling rapidity—human learning is frequently obsolete and does not fit either the person who applies it or the situation in which the behavior takes place. People in the helping professions therefore frequently face patients or clients who apply what they have learned and suffer because of the obsolescence of such learning. Psychiatrists, clinical psychologists and social workers are then tempted to engage the patient in a process of unlearning which is frequently termed "working through" or "confrontation" or "gaining insight." Unfortunately, it is questionable whether such a process of unlearning can ever succeed and whether learning is really extinguishable. First of all, there is the learning dilemma which conceptualizes that the learning of the good interferes with the learning of the better. Even more important is the tendency of the human being to seek earlier forms of gratification in times of stress. Since life, particularly the lives of people seeking help, is apt to be very stressful, clients will be permanently at the risk of regression and frequently found to be yielding to it.

It would seem to be practical, therefore, if members of the helping profession would be satisfied with enabling people to acquire additional learning and thus to provide them with alternatives in coping.

The acquisition of new coping patterns will be found to improve self-image and to give the relief from helplessness by having options of behavior. On the other hand, to destroy a person's learning is, by implication, partial destruction of the self and therefore disturbing to the self-image of the client. This, of course, implies that the helper should have imagination regarding the options of behavior open to a client. This does not imply imposition of change but rather an opening of a panorama of possibilities which may have been unavailable to a person in trouble.

This is only an application of an Aristotelian principle that the physician must have a mental picture of health much as an architect must have a mental picture of a house, and a protection against thoughtlessness under the cover of being nonjudgmental. The helper must have ideas for the client and not wait for the client to have ideas. Whether the client accepts these ideas and can carry them out, is, of course, another question. To see, the actual potentials in the client which the client does not see in himself is the existentialist requirement in helping.

The Behavior Paradigm

The human organization can be visualized as a disequilibrium—an imbalance between requirements of input and output.[4] Human beings require the intake of food and the elimination of waste products. They require association and dissociation. One needs people but can have too many people in one's life. One needs to form relationships and to terminate relationships—these processes go on ceaselessly during life. We call them needs and find that we become aware of them only when they have remained unsatisfied beyond normal times of satisfaction. We get hungry at meal times. We need people after we have been lonely. We need rest after activity. The reverse is also true.

We speak of drive signifying a need activated by continued lack of satisfaction. The concept of drive is linguistically powerful because it suggests loss of autonomy. One cannot think of anything else. One must find satisfaction of this need. One must omit other pursuits. One is being driven. Drive, however, implies direction and direction is usually indicated by experience of the satisfaction of such drives in the past. The experience of drive combines with recall. The recall of satisfactions previously encountered and the seeking of them again is conceptualized as goal setting. The combination of drive and goal is called motivation and suggests that people must move to find their satisfactions. Behavior, therefore, is essentially goal-directed movement because the satisfactions which we pursue in our goals are hardly ever at hand, they are hardly ever readily available. The wisdom of our language reveals this essential part of the human condition in such terms as going for dinner, going to bed, going to school, going to have fun, etc. Only in infancy or in disabling sickness are things being brought to us. The experience of getting satisfaction in passivity is therefore strategically placed at the beginning of life and hardly ever fully abandoned. It is embedded in the fairy tale of fried chicken flying into your mouth; it is also experienced in massage; and it is experienced as a secondary gain in sickness. Because of the tendency to regress when under stress, people who need help will be hoping to have things done for them, to be spared the activities which lead to needed satisfaction. How this can be overcome will be discussed later on in this book when we discuss techniques of helping. Suffice it to say here that human beings must have the capacities to make contact with need-satisfiers, with the reality behind their goals. This, however, is not enough. They must also have the ability to consume what the need-satisfier has to offer. Food has to be chewed and swallowed, the love and care that a human being has to offer must be received rather than rejected, dates have to be enjoyed, books read, etc. Failure in human behavior can therefore be due either to the nonexistence of reality behind the goals or to the inability to use the reality with which contact has been made. Everyone knows the anger of the person who finds a restaurant closed when he wants to have dinner there; the anger when you want a drink and find the refrigerator defrosted. Everybody knows the discomfort and anger of being stood up, or the disappointment in finding your food unappetizing, your drinks stale or your date unpleasant. The outcome of behavior can therefore be rewarding or non-rewarding, and the consequences of either have to be considered.

If you were an animal, preferably an experimental rat, and your behavior was rewarded, you would probably show signs of tension-reduction and desist from further activity. You might curl up and go to sleep. The human being, however, is more complex. When one drive is satisfied, human perception may be free for another drive. Behavior may change direction but may not come to an end. Furthermore, every human act consumes irrevocably the time devoted to it. In consequence, there is loss implied even in successful behavior—the loss of satisfactions which could have been obtained if time had been devoted to pursuits other than the one actually sought. Young people are unaware of this utilization of time because they feel they have time unending for the attainment of their goals. This unrealistic perspective is being corrected in later life, usually when it is too late to reassign priorities. It may therefore be an important function of the helping process to protect the client against nonuse of time.

A patient or slow-moving therapist may actually rationalize his own passivity as methodology and thus become an ally to the client's non-use of time.

If behavior is nonsuccessful, we have different consequences. First of all, there is an increase in tension rather than tension reduction. Drives are not extinguished by starvation. In addition to this, the experience of failure as such affects the self-image. The unsuccessful person creates a new need, conceivably of drive character, namely, the need for psychological repair. A narcissistic wound has been inflicted, a self-image has been damaged or damage previously suffered confirmed. Therefore, the helper must aid the client not only in finding new coping patterns but also in improving his self-evaluation. Here he comes in conflict with our puritanical heritage which equates success with personal worth. He must convey to the client what the Greeks have known—namely, that suffering ennobles, that suffering confirms man's humanity, makes him more alive, and ultimately presents a challenge rather than a defeat. In Western civilization where the presentation of Christ on the Cross signifies the ascent of humanity to divinity, the idea of the dignity of suffering should not be difficult to convey.

VARIOUS TYPES OF NEEDS

In the preceding section we have made frequent reference to organic needs such as food and drink, rest and activity, elimination and sex. We have also made reference to man's character as an open system. Since man is not self-sufficient, all these needs, particularly in early life, require the ministration of others. The essential discomfort of human beings is loneliness. We inflict loneliness on children as punishment by sending them to their room, on adult persons by putting them into solitary confinement. Next to capital punishment, the infliction of loneliness is one of the greatest threats to man. People in distress may have many associates but none who has the time, understanding or skill to help them in their suffering. In that context they will feel lonely. We should therefore say that relief of loneliness in their battle with distress is the first requirement of people in need of help.

It is also part of the organic equipment of human beings that they develop, mature and decline. Man grows from helplessness into strength and returns to helplessness. Through most stages of his development, a person needs the experience of growing strength and in the years of decline, of maintenance or slowdown of his abilities; the essential needs which clients present will be the needs to combat loneliness and helplessness. Loneliness can be fought in part by the establishment of the helping relationship. The removal of helplessness, however, is trickier and requires additional effort. No client wants to be alone, but many clients may be ambivalent about their helplessness. An infant's paradise of satisfied dependency is never fully overcome and is sought again in periods of stress. For this reason, almost all helping is a struggle—a struggle between the maturation-enhancing or maturity-preserving goal of the helper and the regressive goal-seeking of the client. This task is complicated by the ambivalence of the worker who, under the stress of being a professional helper, may develop regressive tendencies himself through which he unconsciously and defensively becomes an ally of the regression of the client. Helping is, therefore, a struggle not only with the client but also with the ambivalence of the helper. It is a two-front battle.

REFERENCES

1. Tamotsu Shibutani, *Society and Personality,* Prentice-Hall, 1961 Englewood Cliffs, N.J., 1961, p. 64.
2. Paul Watzlawick, "A Review of the Double Bind Theory" in *Communication, Family and Marriage,* Don D. Jackson, ed., Palo Alto, California, Science and Behavior Books, Vol. 1, 1968, pp. 63-86.
3. Robert Waelder, *Introduction to the Living Thoughts of Freud,* New York, Longmans Green, 1941, pp. 3-4.
4. Muzafer Sherif, *An Outline of Social Psychology,* New York, Harper & Bros., 1948, pp. 11ff, 19ff.

CHAPTER III

INTERACTION
AND THE
EXCHANGE PRINCIPLE

|Since human beings are open systems, they require input and output for life maintenance and reproduction. Much of the input and output takes place in the form of exchanges between human beings./The infant is fed by the mother. The child's thriving presents the mother with an input supplying her deficit of reassurance that she is an adequate mother. The smiling response[1] is another output of the child in exchange for the input provided by the turning to the child of a smiling adult. In the act of intercourse, the input of semen by the male is exchange for the output of vaginal secretion by the female, and so forth.

| Purely physiological exchanges are elaborated in the course of development by psychological exchanges. The primary psychological needs of the human being based on his experience of dependency are the need for association and the need to overcome helplessness] It can be presumed generally that the presence of one human being is an exchange for the presence of another human being, but it requires some analysis to distinguish the associations which are strengthening from those which are not. Returning to the existentialist concept of care even in association, one can observe distance and closeness. Body language and positioning reveal whether people experience their association as comforting or strengthening, whether they want to maintain or bring it to an end, or whether they can

17

take it only under restricting conditions, maintaining their own territories from which the other is excluded even in association.

In the dimension of helplessness, exchanges can relate to objects, such as gifts, to thought content, such as information, or to feelings, such as expressions of love, hate, anger or tenderness. These exchanges reassure the persons involved that they are worth being sustained by objects, fed information or love, or at least considered important enough to be hurt physically or emotionally. Every notice taken of the other is a message to him that he is important. Only when no notice is taken is the exchange refused, and the self-image of the other negatively affected.

The proposition that exchanges of love and exchanges of information enhance the self-image will strike most people as self-evident. That this happens also in apparently hurtful exchanges, however, may require further elaboration. The needs of human beings can be classified as libidinal and constructive or aggressive and destructive. Actually there seems to be a disequilibrium between love and hate in every human being which is permanently changing according to which is gratified and which is not. It is common experience that many people make up after a quarrel and that sex is frequently better after a fight than it is without such a release of hostility. This makes perfect sense in terms of the behavior paradigm according to which satisfaction of one drive sets the human organism free for the experience of another drive. The legitimacy of destruction and aggression is only obscured by the value system of the Judeo-Christian tradition and by the apprehension that unlimited destruction might put an end to life or severely impair its maintenance and developmental potential. Although the wisdom of the language seems to suggest that one can be "smothered by love," anxiety seems to be tied to destruction more than to love. The concept of destruction itself implies irreversibility and, as such, reawakens feelings of helplessness and thus needfulness rather than need-satisfaction. It is almost always overlooked that every act of consumption implies a measure of destruction. One has to chew one's food in order to make it digestible, recast information in order to make it part of one's own orientation, reinterpret messages of feelings that another person sends in order to find them acceptable and manageable.

Therefore, human exchanges are in a measure always disappointing. What has been given does not live up to the expectation of the recipient and is changed in the act of reception from what is was intended to be by the giver.

The exchange principle as here presented does not fit too well into Homans' "Payoff Matrix" which implies a profit experience and therefore one who is a loser and one who is a gainer.[2] In human affairs it is better to think in terms of an equity principle which is determined by the question, "Do I get enough?", rather than by the question, "Do I get more than I give?" The comparison is not with the exchange benefit of the other at the same moment of time but with the exchange benefit for oneself between past and present.

It is frequently heard that marriage is a "50-50 proposition." This implies that the getting and giving of one is compared with the getting and giving of the other. Where such comparisons are made, the outcome must be unsatisfactory for at least one interactor and probably indicates an unsatisfactory marriage because the dissatisfaction of one will be conveyed to the other. If the question, however, is asked, "Do I get *enough* out of my marriage?", many people will find a satisfactory answer.

There are many categories of obstacles to satisfactory exchanges. Perhaps the outstanding one is distance based on difference which makes it difficult for two people in interaction to identify the deficits and surpluses of the other. The differences between male and female, young and old, white and black come easily to mind as the reasons for misperception regarding the need system of the other in an interactional relationship. In all such situations the naive question, "Why are you not more like me?", is silently raised and prevents the person who raises the question from coming closer. Differences, however, can also be seen and more fruitfully so as resources in a storehouse of gratification which might meet one's own deficit. In that respect, all helping is an overcoming of distance and difference between the helper and the person to be helped. A difference frequently increases by the very fact of professional training in one of the helping professions. To know more than somebody else is an institutionalization of such distance and difference. Consequently, the helper must learn to overcome the distance which his learning has produced. Since one cannot really give up one's professional training, one can only decrease the distance of the client or patient by sharing the results of such training with him and permitting him to change it for his own use.

Exchanges can also be obstructed by similar changes in needfulness. Two persons who have the same needfulness cannot satisfy one another—two starving people cannot feed one another. Unfortunately, it is very seductive to look for satisfaction to him who seems to need it. Particularly in marriages, one frequently finds young people tying themselves to one another because they sense their own suffering in the other. Two patients, however, do not one therapist make.

Another obstruction to exchange is a symbolic meaning that people have for one another. Spouses often represent parents to one another; for students, teachers; and for employees, executives may do the same. The transfer of feelings which were legitimate in the relationship of parent and child, however, obstructs the exchange principle in the spouse relationship because the sexual relationship is put under the incest taboo of the parent-child relationship. The transfer of feelings that a child has for a parent may lead him to have expectations which a teacher cannot satisfy in a student nor an executive in an employee.

Ultimately, inequity in a relationship where one gets enough but the other too little may, in the long run, so deplete the one who gives enough that he suddenly feels that he can give no more. This is probably the reason for the unexpected ending of long-term relationships. People always wonder why marriages that have lasted twenty-five years or longer should end in divorce and why friendships of long standing should turn sour. The answer is probably that a dependent person has so depleted the person who met his dependency-needs that the other can no longer sustain the relationship. In the long run the phenomenon of complimentarization[3,4], according to which a person with a strong need stimulates another person to satisfy this need seems to produce a breakdown of the relationship.

What is most frequently exchanged, however, are ambivalences. People want to give and want to hold on. Exchanges usually take place when the ambivalences are resolved which makes the resolution of ambivalence one of the key tasks of helping. Unfortunately, it is a great professional risk that the ambivalance of the client or patient stimulates the ambivalence in the professional helper. Developmental arrests in a client may stimulate developmental regression in the professional. It is seductive to revisit one's own developmental fantasies by listening to the developmental fantasies of the client. Such listening may become a secondary gain in the helping, but it may obstruct the resolution of ambivalence in the worker about letting the client go or helping him to learn other options or more age-appropriate behavior. It thus turns into a problem of termination which frequently presents greater problems to the helper than to the person who is to be helped.

REFERENCES

1. René A. Spitz, *The First Year of Life,* New York, International Universities Press, 1965, pp. 88-97.

2. George Caspar Homans, *Social Behavior,* New York, Harcourt-Brace-Jovanovich, 1961, 1974, pp. 51-52.
3. Robert Waelder, "The Scientific Approach to Casework" in *Personality,* Clyde Kluckhohn and Henry A. Murray, eds., New York, A. A. Knopf, Inc., 1950, pp. 531-539.
4. Robert Waelder, *Basic Theory of Psychoanalysis,* New York, International Universities Press, 1960, p. 107.

CHAPTER IV

THE NEEDS OF THE HELPER AND THE CLIENT OR PATIENT

As has been said previously, the basic human conditions requiring relief are helplessness and loneliness. Although it would appear that these needs are only experienced by the recipient of help, they are also—in different form and in different degree—experienced by the professional helper. Observation of the exchange principle, therefore, suggests a *prima facie* absurdity, namely an exchange of two deficits between the two interactors in the helping process. Since it is the basic assumption that in a successful human interaction the surplus of one must meet the deficit of the other, we are faced with a paradox which requires solution.

As concerns loneliness, the client has experienced this in the sense that there is no scheduled time in which he can count on another to keep him company in his misery. Parents and teachers may be impatient with children, spouses may have their own worries and may not be ready to empathize with the worries of the other, and friends may have to go about their business when one needs them. The company which the person in misery needs, however, must be predictable and secure. It is the scheduled appointment which gives the person requiring help the security of being attended to at a predictable point in time and, in psychiatry and social work, for a predictable period of time. On the other side, loneliness of the professional helper is relieved by persons seeking his help. Again, the scheduled appointment brings the assurance of predictable client company. The coming of the client relieves the doubt about being needed, about being professionally occupied and being acknowledged as competent. The scheduled time gives the assurance of structure to the professional day. What appeared to be an encounter between two deficits reveals itself as a meaningful exchange between two availabilities for an encounter that is needed on both sides.

That the worker's needs are fulfilled by the client in this respect can be seen by the reaction of a professional helper to "the broken appointment." If the client does not show up, it may mean that he has not been helped, has lost hope for help to come, dislikes the helper, that his anxieties have been aroused beyond the point of tolerance, or that his hostility is being directed at the professional helper as a target. At any rate, the professional helper's need to have the company of a client or patient at the appointed time has been frustrated. Conversely, when a professional does not keep an appointment or lets a client or patient wait, the latter has an experience of rejection.

The same is frequently true when the professional goes on a vacation, or is ill and cannot see people. In such cases preparation of the client or patient is necessary. This gives an experience of sharing in the planning of the separation.

It is one of the great obstacles in establishing a relationship between clinic patients and physicians that the gatekeepers of the medical service— the receptionists and appointment secretaries—frequently overschedule the professional or schedule clients at the same time. This enforced waiting leaves the person who comes for help with the experience of inferiority, rejection and "an unscheduled period of loneliness" in which he can do nothing but wait and dwell on his misery or, at best, read much-used magazines he otherwise would not have read which makes him feel that he is wasting time. The writer has observed from his own waiting for appointments that his doing professional work such as reading examination papers or making notes from scientific magazines brought along in anticipation of the delay somehow disoriented the receptionist. Apparently, this is not expected patient behavior—patients are supposed to do nothing but wait. Otherwise they exhibit independence of behavior and management of time which does not fit into the expectations receptionists have of patient behavior in the waiting room.

The experience of helplessness also takes different forms in the client and in the professional helper. The client's helplessness needs hope that things can get better, that there are other ways of handling his situation which are available to him, and that it won't cost too much money or time. It is important, therefore, to convey to the person seeking help early in the contact[1] —preferably at the first meeting—hope that something can be done, to inject optimism into the situation and an element of confidence that change will not be too expensive in either pain, money, or time. This requires at least a tentative agreement on the goals of the helping process, on the time period required, and on the nature and intensity of discomfort that can be expected in the process of change.[2,3,4,5]

Correspondingly, helplessness on the side of the professional helper is partly temperamental and partly experiential. It is a common experience that the best way of turning a psychiatric resident into a therapeutic nihilist is to give him a series of difficult cases. If one is to convey optimism, one must have optimism. Such optimism can best be produces by a training process which builds helping success into the training experience. As has been pointed out in another connection, the professional helper must have imagination and see options of behavior and experience for the client that the latter does not see for himself. Most important, where feasible, he should have had the experience of having overcome what the client or patient needs to overcome. The setting of a limited period for the helping process either by calender or by the number of therapeutic encounters also protects the professional helper against his need of prolonging the contact for reasons of counter-transference, for economic determinants, because he has grown fond of the client and of the relationship with him, or because of his own need for stability in professional work. The problem of termination is frequently harder for the helper than for the person to be helped.

Perhaps most important, the professional helper must control his ambition for the improvement of the client. It is sometimes difficult for a social worker, marriage counselor, clinical psychologist or a psychiatrist to understand that a person's discomforts may have become part of his identity or at least part of a cathectic familiarity which the client cannot or does not want to give up. The question must always be asked, "How much change is the client willing to undergo for the disappearance of this discomfort?" This has frequently been implied in the term "limited goals," but these have usually been defined as consideration of reality-factors such as age, available social alternatives, or levels of education and training, and have not been sufficiently seen as dynamic limitations of growth and development in the process of helping.

A more invidious need of the professional helper in psychiatry and social work is the need to reexperience the secondary gains of the client, to revisit the child in himself, as it were, and to retard the client's growth by his ambivalence about his own development. The writer has often marveled about this factor in the selection of development-related specialties. Why does one want to become an adolescent psychiatrist, a child psychiatrist? Why do college students so frequently profess a preference for working with emotionally disturbed children? One would be inclined to think that a physician who has gone through psychiatric training would have achieved enough personal maturity to prefer work with adults. One would be inclined to assume that young people who have made it to college age would be glad not to be forced back into contacts with childhood. It is a tempting hypothesis to suggest that these professional choices or professional aspirations are really wishes to find a professional role which permits a return to preoccupation with developmental difficulties which have not been fully worked out or overcome. Obviously, a patient engaged in a therapeutic contact with such a professional will be at grave risk of being victimized by the ambivalence of the therapist about growth. If a social worker, psychologist or a psychiatrist who has not solved his own conflicts about sexuality likes to listen to the sexually acting-out adolescent, what chance is there that the conflict will be resolved by the client rather than being maintained in a repetitive non-helpful sequence?

The need of the professional helper for information always interferes with the need of the patient or client for privacy. Being interviewed, being examined or being observed in the helping process, always implies a nonreciprocated exposure. You undress physically or psychologically before a person who keeps his clothes on or actually fortifies his being clothed by a white coat, a white uniform, or a position behind a desk or a couch. This is perhaps best exemplified by the experience of a patient in a pelvic or prostatic examination. The invasion of privacy cannot but affect the self-image of the patient. The questions of the patient or client whether the professional helper is married, whether he has had similar experiences or what his state of health is are futile attempts of the person seeking help to reestablish human dignity through mutuality of information. In this he encounters the affective neutrality of the helper.[6] It has sometimes been questioned whether a patient is not entitled to know something about his doctor, or a client about his social worker.

It should be considered, however, that an exchange of the privacy of the helper for the privacy of the person to be helped would not be an equitable exchange. In the helping process the patient or client gives his privacy only once and to only one person or, in group or in gestalt therapy, to a few persons. A professional helper who would give his privacy to all his patients or clients would have to give it so often that he would have no privacy left. It would become public and thus, ultimately, nonreciprocal. The whole proposition brings unhappy memories of the temple prostitutes in religious cults in which intimacy was offered indiscriminately to the worshipers.

What a client or patient can, however, rightfully claim in lieu of such exchange of intimacy is legitimation of the invasion of his privacy through information. Why must the social worker, psychiatrist, physician or nurse have this information? The client or patient has need to know *what* the interview or the examination is supposed to reveal that would be helpful to the helper in the helping process and *why* it would be helpful. Here we come up against a special problem of linguistics. Physicians and lawyers are trained in a long tradition to express their information in a professional language which draws heavily on Latin and Greek and uses English mostly for connecting words. They therefore face a task of translation which has an unfortunate by-product of status-diminution. If you can say what you have learned in your professional training in a language which John Doe can understand, you give up the sacredness of your information. The professional need to keep the sacred secret, works against communication with the patient and leaves the invasion of his privacy either threatening or offensive. However, this is the only way which the author can see as an equitable exchange of information between helper and client. If you must tell me about yourself, I must tell you why I need to know. If you must show yourself to me, I must tell you why I want to see. Of course such exchanges will remain incomplete on both sides. A professional may fear that full information about the nature of the professional inquiry may be too threatening to the client and may even interfere with the usefulness of gathering the information. A patient or client may consciously or unconsciously withhold pertinent information. The answer does not lie in the completeness of the exchange but in the experience of the exchange. It is not the totality of the information which is essential, but that the information be given by both sides. If quantity of information is the question, then the answer must be adequacy rather than fullness.

One of the needs of the professional helper that seems to gain increasing attention in medical and social work circles is a type of practice which is in harmony with the conception of the morality of the helper. In the medical field this need is expressed in controversies around such questions as telling the patient the truth about his terminal condition, protecting his interests in clinical research, prolonging organic life where mental life seems to have ceased, total cardiac replacement, and the problem of abortion.[7] Less frequently mentioned but also troublesome is the maintenance of professional standards where their time-demands conflict with the work-demands of the practitioner. Selection of patients for dialysis quite often presents difficult problems. To be conflicted about the morality of professional procedures, however, poses another problem of morality for physician—namely, the moral responsibility to come to a reasoned decision and not drift into procedures where he meets minimal institutional resistance. Conceptions of morality may differ from person to person, from specialty to specialty, from religious denomination to religious denomination, and ultimately from institutional setting to institutional setting. What medicine, however, must ask from its practitioners is a moral stance which puts the interest of the patient above the interest of the professional.

This represents a special problem in social work where students are trained to be nonjudgmental in their interactions with clients and not impose their values upon the person who seeks their help. Psychiatry faces a similar problem, particularly since there is an increasing shift from patients who seek help to patients assigned for help. Formerly this was essentially the case with children brought by their parents for treatment. Now it is true for sex offenders, drug abusers, alcoholics and members of violent gangs. In all these instances the question could be raised as to whether a psychiatrist or social worker has the right to treat a client or patient who does not want to be treated—to force middle-class values upon a young man who has grown up absorbing the survival standards of a gang culture, to force a person who uses drugs either as a status device or as an escape, not to do that, and the same is true for the alcoholic. When one abandons high levels of abstraction and looks into the concreteness of the life-situation of such people, the desirability of treatment-goals which would change their condition seems to be less problematical than it may first appear. A reasonably good definition of treatment-goal will probably be perceived in most of these instances. Where a psychiatrist or social worker cannot find desirability of change in such situations, it might well be his professional and moral obligation to step aside and accept neither private nor public money for a service he feels should not be rendered.

There is, however, a more troublesome problem of morality not so much in treatment-goals but in the selection of a treatment technique. The problem probably lies most frequently in a lack of fit between what one has learned in professional schools and what one feels one is able to do. Here institutional constraints may produce severe moral conflict. Training and supervision in and by themselves may confront professional people with the demands of the application of techniques to which they are resistant or which they have outgrown. It is the pervasive thesis of this book that morality as well as efficiency would require that no professional helper should yield to institutional constraints which make him do what he thinks should not be done or what he thinks he cannot do.

One of the most troublesome needs of social workers is the resolution of the conflict between a strongly felt need to change the social systems from which their clients suffer and job requirements which force them into helping processes which leave these social systems unattacked. This is probably most strongly felt in public welfare where the daily confrontation with poverty and the inadequacy of the public-assistance allowance seem to put the social worker into a troubled alliance with taxpayers and the social class system. Working with minority clients such as Blacks, Chicanos, and American Indians accentuates this conflict. In recent times the Women's Movement has probably contributed to the awareness of the dilemma. Case workers and group workers feel that they should devote their energies to advocacy and policy-making. Social workers engaged in advocacy feel that case workers and group workers apply "Band-aids" where surgery would be indicated. Community organization workers seem to have found an activity which comes closest to social change short of revolution; still they feel the threat of corruption that seems to follow from the threat of being co-opted by the system. Obviously it is difficult to take a salary from a system that one feels should not be permitted to exist. Race- and sex-consciousness add to the difficulty. Black social workers are conflicted about working within a white-majority-dominated system. Women feel similarly threatened by working in male-dominated organizations. In this period of history, Social workers are suffering from the incongruity of being ideally identified with revolution and practically serving the system.[8]

This difficulty has distinctly historical roots. The settlement movement was started by upper-middle class men and women. The Fabians in England were middle-class people who felt deeply the injustice of the system to which they belonged. Even the professional designation as social workers indicated the alliance with the disadvantaged and an antagonism to the people of wealth who financed the profession. The difficulty has been accentuated by changes in the curricula in schools of social work which have turned increasingly to the study of social problems and social policy and, thus, withdraw faculty resources and prestige from the training for the modalities of helping—counseling and leading discussion or activity groups in which many graduates must still find employment.

Thus, in a subtle way we find social workers not only burdened by conflict between ideology and practice but also by a disparity between training and job demand.

The solution seems to lie in directing the skills of dyadic helping to systems-change. Ultimately all helping is dyadic because it is the biological destiny of man to engage in face-to-face relationships in bringing about change. Social workers in the school system probably will have the easiest way of problem solution by applying the dynamics of helping to dyadic encounters with administrators as well as those with students and parents. Medical social workers may find similar opportunities in hospitals and health centers. The public assistances, however, will present difficulties for such approaches to systems-change because the social worker has no organizational contact with legislators on whom the redistribution of income depends. Ultimately social workers will have to find the conflict solution in advocacy, lobbying or intrapsychic remedies such as gaining perspective about the impact that individual activity has upon social change. In this respect it might be pointed out that the philosophical wisdom of Aristotle as well as that of Moses Maimonides has suggested a middle position as the essence of morality—rejecting excessive engagement in what often seems to be desirable.

REFERENCES

1. Helen Harris Perlman, "Intake and Some Role Considerations" in *Social Casework in the Fifties,* Cora Kasius, Ed., Family Service Association of America, 1962, pp. 163-174.
2. Martin T. Orne and Paul H. Wender, "Anticipatory Socialization for Psychotherapy: Method and Rationale", *American Journal of Psychiatry,* Vol. 124, (9, March 1968), pp. 88-98.
3. Julie Jessie Taft, Ed., *Counseling and Protective Service as Family Casework: A Functional Approach,* Philadelphia, Pennsylvania School of Social Work, 1946, pp. 83-94.
4. Florence Hollis, *Casework - A Psychosocial Therapy,* New York, Random House 1964, pp. 205-207.
5. William G. Nagel, "A Student Worker's Use of a New Definition of a Private Prison Society's Structure to Strengthen the Sponsorship of a Man on Parole", *The Prison Journal,* Vol. XXVIII, No. 3, July, 1948, pp. 409-421.

6. Talcott Parsons, *The Social System,* New York, Free Press of Glencoe, 1951, p. 343.
7. Renée C. Fox, "Ethical and Existential Developments in Contemporaneous American Medicine: Their Implications for Culture and Society," *Milbank Memorial Foundation Quarterly,* Health and Society, Fall 1974, pp. 445-483.
8. Daniel Thursz, "Social Action as a Professional Responsibility," *Social Work,* Vol. 11, No. 3 (July 1966), pp. 12-21; George A. Brager, "Advocacy and Political Behavior," *Social Work,* Vol. 13, No. 2, April 1968, pp. 5-15; Mary J. McCormick, "Social Advocacy: A New Dimension in Social Work," *Social Casework,* Vol. 51, No. 1, Jan. 1970, pp. 3-11.

CHAPTER V

INSTRUMENTALITIES
OF HELPING

Part I

In the perspective of time, a process seems to have occurred which could be conceptualized as deconcretization in helping. In the Scriptures we encounter the ethical command to farmers to leave one-tenth of their crop unharvested, to be taken by the poor. In Roman times the poor were given bread and shows by the imperian government. In the Middle Ages royalty and Church distributed alms. Only in modern times has the giving of material support been largely replaced by emotional and interactional restructuring aimed at helping the person in misery to cope more effectively with his condition. In the late 1960's and early 1970's even the idea of personality change, abstract as it was in comparison to the giving of material help, has been replaced by the more abstract and more radical idea of social change.

Parallel with this process of deconcretization, a process of specialization has gone on which demands ever higher skills of the helper to the point where the skill itself is more important than the humanity of the helper. This is particularly manifested in the development of medicine in this century in which the general practitioner has been replaced by the specialist. Very few persons would prefer a neurosurgeon with a good personality to a neurosurgeon with an unpleasant personality who has greater experience.

These developments have required professionalization,[1] and in deconcretized helping, training of the helper in the handling of his own personality as an instrument of bringing about personality change and in the acquisition of skills not accessible to the layman. In essence, the process has been turned away from helping that everyone can do to helping which only specially-trained people can do. As mentioned in Chapter I, an apparent exception to this rule is the entrance of paraprofessionals into legal and community mental health work but, even there, the need of in-service training is recognized and met by special seminars and institutes.

All requirements of special training have produced distance between the helper and the person to be helped and have thereby created new problems in helping. The current instrumentalities of helping such as casework,[2] group work,[3] psychotherapy,[4] psychoanalysis[5] and the medical interventions of surgery and medication therefore face a problem of overcoming distance created by training. One of the means of decreasing this distance is communication and the expression of respect for suffering. As a broad generalization it could be said that professional helpers are more skillful in the expression of respect for suffering than they are in communicating with the client or patient. It has been pointed out in the preceding chapter that professionals tend to guard their professional language or technical jargon as an anchor point of identity, as a "sacred trust", and feel reluctant to or incapable of transfering their professional knowledge into lay terms. It would then appear that one of the instrumentalities requiring increased attention in the future is the development of a means of communication which makes the person to be helped a partner in rather than a recipient of helping.

By and large, one can still separate medicine from social work by a difference in the means of helping. Social workers use foremost their personality and their interactional skills as instrumentalities while physicians and nurses use mostly physical interventions as illustrated by the giving of medication and surgery as therapeutic instrumentalities. A middle position is being taken by psychiatry which uses the provision of interpersonal experience as well as psychotropic drugs as instrumentalities. The emphasis of medicine on skillful interventions of a technical and tangible nature will probably be further enhanced by the increasing bureaucratization of medical services. Bureaucratization implies labor turnover and depersonalization of the service. Physicians rotate, as do nurses, physical and occupational therapists. Where constancy of professional relationship cannot be expected, skillful material intervention must become the essential instrumentality of the helping process. Social workers, psychiatrists and other therapists working with dyadic skills are more dependent on the constancy of the professional relationship as an instrumentality.

The use of any instrumentality has its own drawbacks which the professional helper must try to minimize. People find it difficult to accept money even when they need it badly. They suffer in their self-image if they cannot reciprocate. They feel that they violate the exchange principle in human affairs. It has frequently been observed that ex-prisoners who receive monetary assistance from social agencies to bridge them over the first time of transition from institutional maintenance to personal maintenance, find it physically difficult to take the money being offered to them. Most people know the difficulty and resistance experienced when writing "thank you" letters after receiving a gift. Beggers in Central European countries acknowledge the receipt of a coin not with the equivalent of our "thank you," but with a sentence calling on God to reward the giver.

The social work ideal of helping the client to help himself is therefore not only an idealization which fits into the American value system of independence but is a protection of the client against the offense of being helped totally by another.

A clinical conference in which the patient is consulted serves similar purposes. It is frequently overlooked that being a patient in a hospital implies a status-deterioration most people find difficult to experience. The "crock" is essentially a patient who insists on retaining his status. Medical intervention may be made technically easier by reducing the patient to helplessness and unquestioning obedience, but it often produces a psychological reaction which may make the experience of medical intervention a negative one. This might account for the hostility which the medical helping professions (physicians, nurses, physical therapists, laboratory technicians, etc.) frequently encounter.

Both the use of the self as an instrumentality of helping and the depersonalization of the patient in the service of technical efficiency produce problems for the helper. It is exceedingly difficult for social workers and psychiatrists not to experience a restimulation of personal problems that have been overcome. It is difficult to listen to an account of parent-child conflict without remembering one's own. No marriage is frictionless and listening to the account of a marital conflict is likely to produce in the professional helper thoughts and feelings about his own marriage. Physicians and nurses who encounter the hostility of the depersonalized patient will reciprocate with hostility. The contact with the dying patient will stimulate their own death anxieties. It is therefore an essential instrumentality of helping to learn keeping one's own life out of the reaction to and concern with the person to be helped. The classical example of such a failure in using oneself as an instrumentality in helping is the phenomenon of counter-transference where the psychoanalyst, stimulated by the transference of the patient, reacts to him with feelings he in turn has experienced in relation to others but not in relation to the patient. This is an instrumentality which nonprofessional helpers have not learned to build into their efforts of helping.

Another instrumentality of helping is the use of peers in the helping process. Group work, group therapy and Alcoholics Anonymous are outstanding examples of such uses. The experience of fellowship in suffering liberates the person to be helped from the feeling that he alone is cursed. It also helps him to acquire the strength which comes from numbers. Misery shared is misery lightened. It also creates a possibility for therapeutic tendencies to develop in the group members through identification with the group leader whose position is less powerful than that of a therapist in a one-to-one relationship. In group therapy everyone becomes a therapist. The helping model becomes incorporated into the behavior of the client and transfers an experience of competence to the helpless.

In the action groups that have recently attracted the attention of social workers—Welfare Rights Mothers, Women's Liberation and Black Caucuses, an element of separation and an element of action combine to produce an experience of strength which the individual member could not have hoped to attain. This experience is helpful independent of the results of political action attempted. It is the experience of talking back to misery with the vocal strength of a chorus rather than with the whimper of individual lament.

REFERENCES

1. Eliot Freidson, *Profession of Medicine, A Study of the Sociology of Applied Knowledge,* New York, Dodd, Mead & Co. Inc., 1970, pp. 57-63, 69-70, 354.
2. Arthur E. Fink, *et al., The Field of Social Work,*New York, Holt, Rinehart and Winston, Inc., 1963, pp. 68-92; *Child Therapy, A Casework Symposium,* Eleanor Clifton & Florence Hollis, eds., Family Service Association of America, 1948; Florence Hollis, *Casework,* New York, Random House, Inc., 1964.

3. Arthur E. Fink, *op. cit.,* pp. 450-480.

4. E. Lakin Phillips, *Psychotherapy,* A Modern Therapy and Practice, Englewood Cliffs, N.J., Prentice Hall, Inc., 1956; Perry London, *The Modes and Morals of Psychotherapy,* New York, Holt, Rinehart & Winston, Inc., 1964; Rudolf Ekstein, Ph.D. and Robert S. Wallerstein, M.D. *The Teaching and Learning of Psychotherapy,* New York, Basic Books, Inc., 1958; Richard D. Chessick, M.D., *Intensive Psychotherapy,* New York, Jason Aronson, Inc., 1974.

5. *The Basic Writings of Sigmund Freud,* New York Random House, Inc., 1938; Robert Waelder, *Basic Theory of Psychoanalysis,* New York, International Universities Press, 1960.

CHAPTER VI

INSTRUMENTALITIES
OF HELPING
Part II

Students of medicine, nursing, clinical psychology and social work, as well as persons who may consider any of these careers, need a panorama of helping instrumentalities in order to find out what specialty would attract them. Thus, they can reject what may leave them neutral, may bore them, or even potentially make them uncomfortable. This chapter, therefore, represents an attempt to provide such an orientation.

In this format the reader will find various categories of helping among which only one may be congenial to or fit his or her ideological orientation. I suggest therefore that readers take out of the format what seems to present to them their particular "fit." This suggestion reflects my belief that one cannot learn a methodology of helping which is not congenial to one's own personality and one's own social values. One can only elaborate and refine through training a specific potential. This is based partly on a genetic accident such as a congenital activity or passivity pattern, partly on one's idiosyncratic development, partly on one's powers of abstraction, partly on one's vulnerability to contacts with the concreteness of disease and suffering and partly on one's cultural orientation as it is derived from the history of the population group to which one belongs and the social setting in which one has grown up.

There are, however, also a few universal requirements which seem to apply to the helping process in medicine and nursing as well as to the helping process in social work. They have been identified by Jules H. Masserman[1] and are presented here in the belief that they will be found useful by every helper independent of his fit for one instrumentality of helping or the other.

Since all helping is a struggle, it might be helpful to classify the areas of helping by the point of attack. It seems proper to them that physicians and nurses choose as such point of attack the body of a patient, that social workers, clinical psychologists and psychiatrists choose his mind and that family therapists and social policy makers have developed strategies of intervention which attack complex systems and choose organizations such as families, departments of welfare, hospitals and health centers. In every one of these categories the helper has the choice between working with singularities or pluralities. He can engage one body in the helping process, one mind, and one family or one school, but he can engage also pluralities such as the bodies of a population—preventive medicine—of a plurality of minds—group therapy—or a plurality of organizations—a plurality of families in network therapy, the welfare system of a state or the health care system of an entire nation. Whenever a helper engages in work with pluralities, he has to be sure that these pluralities have something in common, such as one disease, one type of psychosocial conflict, one type of conflict with the social order, one type of organizational dysfunction, and the like. Without such community of bodily afflication, intrapsychic conflict, deviance or variance and organizational stress, no focused help can be provided for a plurality. Help without focus is no help.

In deciding on a target the helper will have to resolve a conflict between two contradictory tendencies in professional training and professional practice. Specialization is the height of professional accomplishment and a system approach is the professional way of coping with complexity. Specialization implies fractionalization. The medical specialties are frequently based on parts of the body. One becomes a dermatologist, a cardiologist, a urologist, a neurosurgeon or an orthopedic surgeon. If one goes into greater heights of specialization, one becomes a pediatric cardiologist. Similarly, nurses become pediatric nurses, surgical nurses, psychiatric nurses, and the like. Specialization in knowledge and therapy of one organ area, of course, increases competence but it blinds oneself to or at least dims one's awareness of the system to which the organ belongs. The system approach on the other hand prevents the depths of knowledge and skill which specialization permits. One could venture to say that no family therapist can reach the depth of information or help the family members to the depths of information that a psychoanalyst can. One can equally say that no psychoanalyst can have the awareness of the family system in which the patient has to live during or after his analysis without engaging the family in therapeutic sessions in sequence.

The solution of this conflict between the siren call of specialization and the call of the wilderness represented by the system approach can be resolved only in terms of one's own powers of comprehending, encompassing and relating the stimuli presented by the helping situation and by one's vulnerability to concreteness.

This presents, of course, a selective use of the training that any professional school has to offer. School systems by definition must follow a mass approach, standardize what they consider requirements of professional information and skill and permit the students only limited use of discretion in taking the training which seems to fit their personalities. The elaboration of one's own fit into professional development must, therefore, frequently be kept in abeyance until one has freedom of professional choice and professional development. It implies, however, that the self diagnosis of the professional helper is at least as important as the diagnosis of the client or patient. I would even venture to say that the self-diagnosis of the professional helper must be a process continued in every stage of his personal and professional development. Here a change may be indicated by a change in perspective and by the need for relief from professional monotony. Nothing is more deadening than professional routine. In order to revitalize one's professional powers, one may need a change in methodology in order to retain one's level of competence. Change in instrumentality may, therefore, be more helpful to the helper than required by the patient or the client.

According to Masserman, the universalities which every helper may find useful to assume are the "Ur-defenses" of man: first, an illusion of physical invulnerability and possible immortality; second, the hope of brotherly love; and third, a quest for a celestial order. These exalted formulations can be translated into simpler assumptions of universal needs. Except when he goes for a routine physical checkup, no patient or client wants to hear that nothing is wrong with him. The self-diagnosis of the client that he needs help has to be respected. Sending a client or patient away with reassurance is a rejection implying that the call for help was a fool's call. It further implies that symbolic and symptomatic relief has to be given quickly to establish optimism in the process.

The professional helper has to believe the client's judgment that he has enemies or is connected with people who do not give him sufficient love. Since human beings live by exchanges, it is very likely to be true that a person who goes for professional help does not get enough in the human exchange on which he depends. As a matter of fact, a client or patient who assumes full responsibility for his discomfort should be suspected of overdetermined masochism, since it is very unlikely that any person is the sole reason for his own discomfort.

Perhaps most importantly, the client or patient does not want to be treated as trivial. Reference has been made to the fact that he has had this experience already in the waiting room where he is asked to sit down and where his need for prompt contact with the professional helper is being disregarded for purposes of bureaucratic ease. Overscheduling or not being on time for an appointment conveys to the client or patient that his needs for attention can be disregarded with impunity. On a higher level it is important for any sufferer to have a feeling that his existence has meaning in a larger framework. It is important, therefore, to find out in a medical as well as in a social work examination whether the person to be helped has a religious or political affiliation which permits him to transcend his personal destiny. If he does not have such an orientation, the helping experience may be his only chance to gain such meaning. Treating him in the initial stages of the helping process as insignificant is increasing his burden of being alone with his suffering.

REFERENCES

1. Jules H. Masserman, M.D., *Modern Therapy of Personality Disorders,* Dubuque, Iowa, 52001, Wm. C. Brown Company Publishers, 1966, pp. 60-61.

CHAPTER VII

A PANORAMA OF PSYCHOTHERAPIES

In the last chapter the foci of attack that helpers may choose—mind or body, individuals or groups, and organizations or systems—were discussed. This chapter will present a panorama of possible techniques among which those who have chosen the mind as the focus of helping can select their personal fit of intervention. Essentially we are faced with a dichotomy which has been conceptualized by Perry London in his book *The Modes and Morals of Psychotherapy* as psychotherapy and action therapy.[1] Under the concept of psychotherapy, case workers, psychiatrists and psychoanalysts may find a common conceptual shelter and so may, for that matter, Rogerians and Freudians. In psychotherapy the instrument of helping is talk. Psychotherapies are essentially verbal therapies. The primary talker is the client and the therapist is essentially a listener who operates with a bias against sharing his privacy with the client. This does not imply that the silences of the patient are meaningless within the framework of the therapeutic process. They may suggest resistance, depression, hostility, shame, a submission to the value judgments of the therapist who may have given involuntary signals, or simply loyalty to others. Because it is exceedingly difficult to reveal one's self without revealing information about significant other persons in one's life, the silence of the client may reveal his loyalty to others as well as his disloyalty to the therapeutic process. On the other hand, verbal communications from the therapist may have supportive or interpretive purposes and thus form part of the technique, but quantitatively they should be minimal compared with the verbal production of the client or patient. Similarly the silence of the patient should be minimal compared to the silence of the therapist.

Since the main task of speaking rests with the client, he must exercise his options on what he wants to talk about. Strategic maneuvers of the client to shift the responsibility for the selection of topics to the therapist will have to be discouraged by the non-responsiveness of the helper to such maneuvers. It might even be questioned whether interpretations of the thought material of the client should be given by the therapist. Ultimately, interpretation will be convincing and convey a feeling of power to the client only if he himself discovers the connections between his thought work and resultant behavior.

Therefore, one can assume that the modes of psychotherapy essentially require a passive psychotherapist and an active patient. An active therapist and a passive patient would result in a highly unproductive constellation. This fit of the personality pattern of therapist and patient seems to me decisive for a successful use of the instrumentality of psychotherapy in helping. If the therapist is tempted to talk and the patient has a tendency to keep silent, little good will come from the interactive process that is supposed to take place.

The modality and temperamental constellations of psychotherapy have been associated with certain positions in space. In the mode of classic psychoanalysis, the patient is lying on the couch and the psychoanalyst is sitting somewhat behind him so that he can see the patient but the patient cannot see him. In this way the analyst is less tempted to talk and the patient less likely to see the emotions which the therapist shows in reaction to what the patient says. In nonanalytic psychotherapy, however, the therapist and the client face one another at eye level and the temptation for the therapist to talk can be much greater because of the similarity of that situation with everyday dyadic conversations. Furthermore, sitting behind a desk produces an artificial distance between the professional helper and the client which may not be conducive to therapy. It increases the need for self-control on the part of the therapist (case worker and counselor, consulting psychiatrist, minister). He must not yield to the temptation to engage the client in conversation and must not show an emotional engagement in the suffering of the client which would exceed professional concern. Desks also produce difficulties in establishing relationship because they set physical limits to the body language of positioning and thus prevent relationship clues to reach the therapist.

It may now be of interest to know what a Rogerian would say if anything and to compare this with what a Freudian would say if anything. In essence a Rogerian would "reflect" upon a statement of the client by simply repeating it. He might respond to the statement of a client that she hates her husband by saying, "You hate your husband." A Freudian, however, would ask, "Why?" It becomes now clear why the Rogerian intervention is called nondirective.[2] By reflecting on the client's suffering through the instrumentality of repeating his statement, the client is assured of empathic company in his suffering. His self is assured of its worthiness by being reflected upon, and it is thus strengthened and encouraged to expand. The Freudian question "Why?" is directive. It directs the patient to search for causes and, since all causes are associated with the past, it directs him into an historical search, into a rolling back of his developmental history until the discovery of the earlier meaning of an experience illuminates its current meaninglessness and gives the client another choice of conflict resolution.[3] These two modalities suggest two different requirements for the personality of the therapist. The reflection of the Rogerian is essentially accepting, the direction of the Freudian is essentially questioning. As far as it is analytical it is also destructive. This is necessary as the purpose of the Freudian approach is to destroy the armor of a maladaptive development.

On the surface the purpose of psychotherapy could then be stated as being an expansion of the self for the Rogerian, a destruction of misdevelopment and encouragement of more adaptive development for the Freudian. In recent years a third goal-orientation has been proposed by existential psychotherapists who regard the client or patient as an individual who has not used his options for the attainment of authenticity. They try to relieve the resulting suffering by helping him to actualize other potentials of his being for this attainment.[4]

In recent years action therapy under the name of behavior modification has assumed an increasingly competitive stance with psychotherapy. While psychotherapy started in the office of the clinician, action therapy started in the laboratory of the research psychologist. Specifically it takes its theoretical origin from the works of Ivan Pavlov[5] and E. L. Thorndike.[6] It represents a transfer of learning theory from the laboratory to the office of the helper. In the more recent past the instrumentalities of action therapy have become connected with the names of Joseph Wolpe,[7] Andrew Salter[8] and Thomas Stampfl.[9] For these action therapists, observed behavior rather than reported motivation, became the concern of therapy. The mechanisms of behavior replaced the humanism of experience. One could overstate but perhaps exemplify their position by saying that instead of helping to transform an apparently faulty organism into a meaningful human being, they wish to transform the faulty human being into an effective and efficient organism. They are neither affirmative like Rogerians nor inquisitive like Freudians, nor are they concerned with wider systems of meaning like the existentalists. They are concerned with repairing faulty associations between stimuli and responses. Thus, they manipulate behavior in order to eliminate symptoms and find history irrelevant to their task buried in the unconscious.

From this approach follow two strategical conclusions. One, they exercise much greater influence over what happens in the treatment session. Two, they assume responsibility for a specific outcome of treatment. In other words, the activity is essentially theirs and the passivity is assigned to the patient. Again, at the risk of being boring, I would like to stress the need for appropriate temperamental constellations between therapist and patient. A passive therapist and an active patient are obviously ill-suited to this type of therapy. One cannot be a passive-action therapist and one cannot be active when being subjected to behavior modification.

Viewing all behavior as the result of a connection between stimuli and responses, the action therapist sees the patient as exhibiting some unfortunate conditioning, as a person who has learned inappropriate responses to everyday stimuli; in other words, as a person who has learned his symptoms. The task of therapy, therefore, is the identification of unsuitable stimulus response connections, to interfere with them and to establish the conditions for the learning of new and more desirable responses.

For Wolpe all new symptoms are the result of anxiety, and it becomes the task of the therapist to find anxiety-inhibiting responses and to teach the patient to produce these responses regularly when he encounters the stimulus which formerly created anxiety in an uninhibited way. These anxiety-inhibiting responses fall into four categories: conditioned avoidance responses, sexual responses, assertive responses, and relaxation responses. The first ones are anxiety-relief responses, such as saying a specific word to oneself when one feels anxious. For instance, Wolpe teaches his patients to expose themselves to uncomfortable but non-damaging electric shocks and advises them to say the word *calm* when the discomfort becomes too great, whereupon the shocks stop. In this fashion, they experience that saying the word, *calm,* stops discomfort and can generalize the impact of the word *calm* to the discomfort of anxiety. In sexual responses he encourages the patient to look for a person who clearly arouses him and, when in the presence of such a person, to let himself go as circumstances will allow. In specific conditions, this suggests encounters with understanding and experienced prostitutes as a modality of curing impotency in males. In assertive responses, he teaches that angry verbal self-assertion inhibits anxiety and in relaxation responses he helps his patient to a systematic desensitization. He helps his patients to visualize increasingly frightening experiences while being relaxed and to find that a state of relaxation decreases the anxiety.

In essence, what he does, however, is the taking of a careful history which leads him to identify the stimuli which created anxiety in the patient and then exhort the patient to engage in anxiety-inhibiting behavior. He argues the patient into trying exposure to fear while at the same time engaging in relaxation-producing behavior. He thus suggests to the patient to master his body—through mastery of his body, he can master anxiety.

Stampfl represents perhaps one of the most extreme illustrations of a technique of therapy which might be contradictory to the temperaments of many therapists. His implosive actiontherapy works with the assumption that the original association of fright with a stimulus which was wrongly perceived to be hurtful, has gone into repression and been generalized to other stimuli which are equally unhurtful in reality but are not so experienced because the client or patient has learned to reduce his anxiety by escape. Since escape produces tension-reduction, the person never engages in reality-testing and, therefore, never can benefit from extinction. In consequence, Stampfl[10] forces the patient to expose himself to terrifying stimuli which, being only verbal in nature, do not produce physical damage or destruction. In practice he tells the patient every imaginable horror story that his own fantasy can produce. The patient is forced to listen to these horror stories and images while sitting in Stampfl's office and experiences willy-nilly that his anxiety is unrealistic because nothing is happening to him other than the discomfort of listening. In essence he persuades the patient to picture himself in the situation which the therapist describes and believes that since no realization of the frightening imagery occurs, the patient's anxiety will be extinguished and the extinguishing will be generalized to the anxiety formerly created by less frightening stimuli. Stampfl's is not a long drawn-out therapy. He tries to produce utmost terror as soon as possible to produce "an explosion of panic" in the patient. The assumption underlying the therapy, of course, can be stated simply that a person who has been frightened to the utmost and forced to confront the fact that no damage has been done will cease to be frightened by lesser terrors. This therapy is ultimately the most radical application of the principle of extinction derived from learning theory to therapy.

REFERENCES

1. Perry London, *The Modes and Morals of Psychotherapy,* New York, Holt, Rinehart & Winston, Inc., 1964.
2. Carl Rogers, *On Becoming a Person,* New York, Houghton, Mifflin & Co., 1961; Client-Centered Therapy, New York, Houghton, Mifflin & Co., 1965.
3. Robert Waelder, *Basic Theory of Psychoanalysis,* pp. 225ff.
4. *Existential Psychology,* Rollo May, ed., New York, Random House, 1961.
5. Ivan Pavlov, *Lectures on Conditioned Reflexes* Vol. 2, translated and edited by W.H. Gantt, New York, International Publishers, 1941.
6. E.L. Thorndike, *Animal Intelligence,* New York, MacMillan, 1911; *Human Learning,* New York, Century, 1931.
7. Joseph Wolpe, *Psychotherapy by Reciprocal Inhibition,* Stanford, Calif., Stanford University Press, 1958.
8. Andrew Salter, *Conditioned Reflex Therapy: The Direct Approach to the Reconstruction of Personality,* New York, Capricorn Books, Putnam, 1961.
9. Thomas G. Stampfl and Donald J. Levis, "The Essentials of Implosive Therapy: A Learning Theory Based on Psychodynamic Behavioral Therapy," *Journal of Abnormal Psychology,* 1967, Vol. 72, No. 6, pp. 496-503.
10. Thomas G. Stampfl, "Implosive Therapy: Staring Down Your Nightmares," *Psychology Today,* Feb., 1975, pp. 66-73.

CHAPTER VIII

GROUP THERAPY AND FAMILY THERAPY

Having reviewed the various methodologies in dyadic relationships between helper and client, we now must explore the elements of human behavior which come into play when the helper faces groups of clients and turns his being with them, their being with one another, and their being with him, into a therapeutic experience. In 1905 a physician, J. H. Pratt, experimented with a "class method"[1] in motivating patients with pulmonary tuberculosis into observing more carefully the regimen considered therapeutic for their condition. He explained the nature of the disease from which the patient suffered and the working and purpose of the medication and other parts of regimen. He thus practiced the exchange principle which suggests that the doctor has to give of his competence to the patient in return for the patient's efforts involved in submitting to examinations and treatment. Beyond the effect of the exchange principle, competitive factors may well have been at work. Patients called upon to report on their own efforts to get well provided role models for patients who had failed to make such efforts. A reward system was also in effect. Patients who had made progress were placed in the front benches and finally on the platform with the doctors.

The class method was widely adopted by other organically-oriented physicians (Harris,[2] Buck[3] and Chappel[4]) and finally found its entrance into the treatment of patients with neurotic disorders, both adult and children. In the transfer from organic to psychological disorders, however, the class method of instruction had to undergo change. Neurotic disabilities seemed to be resistive to educational and inspirational suggestion and the motivation derived from competitiveness with fellow sufferers. Paul Schilder[5] and Louis Wender[6] introduced psychoanalytic concepts which were applied to the group experience for therapeutic purposes. Topics such as repression, the unconscious, hostility, ambivalence as well as specific constellations of family dynamics were presented to the patients and discussed with them. With the introduction of a psychoanalytic orientation, the patient groups became smaller and free association replaced educational presentation. Schilder particularly identified a number of basic needs which must be uncovered and discussed in group therapy sessions—the need to love and be loved, the tendency to handle and destroy objects and human beings and the tendency to maintain the integrity of one's body.

In the 1940's S.R. Slavson[7] developed a rich body of experience and theory both on activity groups and discussion groups within a therapeutic frame of reference. He concentrated on the importance of establishing criteria for selecting patients and grouping them. As is so frequently the case in the discussion of all therapies, the emphasis was on the patient rather than on the therapist. Although it was undoubtedly true that Slavson developed methodologies which presented a fit with his personality and with the personality of the assistants whom he chose, the warning must be repeated at the risk of monotony that not every social worker or psychiatrist is comfortable in groups or attains intellectual and emotional satisfaction in the diluted experience which every group provides for therapists as well as for the group members. One should also keep in mind that Slavson worked mostly with Jewish patients. It can probably be stated with a certain amount of assurance that at least up to mid-century, Jewish patients presented a host population for pathological inhibitions rather than for pathological acting-out. Still it seems worthwhile to state the principles under which Slavson's group therapy seemed to operate because he was a leader in a new field and because his concepts and ideas may often have validity in other instances. First of all release and catharsis are experienced by the group members and seem to be facilitated by the group process. Ego defenses are weakened and the impulse-life of the group members comes more easily to expression. Transference is greatly facilitated. The group provides an opportunity for change in behavior because it is amorphous and permissive while nontherapeutic groups are usually organized and, as such, tend to lock patients into a specific position of behavioral expectation and social control. Slavson also made a useful distinction between desirable types of group composition according to the nature of the group therapy pursued. He recommended heterogeneity for activity groups and homogeneity of problems for discussion groups.

In historical perspective it is important to note that after mid-century, there was a shift in the character of patients that seemed to fall within the jurisdiction of group therapy. Neurotics were replaced by delinquents, Jewish adolescents by Black adolescents, children who were brought by their parents by juveniles who were assigned by the court system or custodial authorities. It is also interesting to observe in historical perspective how the model for the treatment of neurotic children persisted in the treatment of acting-out and actually or potentially depressed youth. It was perhaps counterproductive to the therapeutic effort to apply an essentially inhibition-resolving methodology to a patient group which seems to resolve its internal conflicts not by suppression or repression of its impulses but by acting them out in the home, in the school and in the streets. In recognition of this possibility, some changes occurred and group therapists suddenly became more directive. They assumed the role of ego-ideals and tried to show the members in the therapy groups that they had technical competence and sources of information which were relevant to the solution of the problems of delinquent youths. Some advocated the use of food as a symbol of the experience of being loved, the spontaneous expression of the therapist's own feelings and the communication of the message that, after all, the delinquents' accustomed ways of conflict-resolution had been found to be counterproductive. Still, a tremendous amount of permissiveness can be observed in leading therapy groups with delinquents. A great amount of exposure to physical threat and an almost unlimited demand on the therapist's patience are required in the modern procedures of group therapy, particularly with adjudicated delinquents. Frequently an especially complicating factor stems from racial differences between patient and therapist and from the conflict between the sub-cultures of therapy and the sub-cultures of custodial care under which these group processes must function. Obviously it is more difficult for a therapist to be a binder than a liberator of impulse-life. The task of group therapy has become much more demanding and much more fraught with risk under the impact of social change. Probably the demands of a fit between the temperament of helper and the methodology of group therapy have become more stringent than they were in the 1940's and 1950's.

The risk which has been frequently described or mentioned in the literature on the practice of group therapy is the seductiveness of play-acting which the situation seems to encourage and to reward. Many group therapists are gratified when the group members participate in discussion. Exhibitionism is thereby encouraged and considered as movement where it actually may be simply an enjoyment of the secondary gains of therapy. Therapists have long been acquainted with the secondary gains of disease and with the secondary gains of the sick role. Perhaps they have not paid sufficient attention to the secondary gains of satisfying primary impulses under the cover of therapeutic effort.

Although pluralities are also involved in therapeutic interventions which attack a system such as the family or a school system, the theory underlying the intervention as well as the dynamics of the intervention process are distinctly different from those underlying group therapy. System theory suggests that one cannot change any part of a system without affecting all its other parts and that these changes will not necessarily all go in the same direction. This was realized probably most clearly in the development of family therapy. In 1945 Mildred Burgum[8]* published a paper which has hardly received the attention it deserves. Entitled, "The Father Gets Worse," it presented the clinical observation that when mother and child improved through child guidance the father, who usually had not been sick, showed increasing signs of disturbances. Similar observations had been made by Bela Mittelmann[9]* who reported, at roughly the same time in the *Psychoanalytic Quarterly* that in the course of psychoanalysis with one spouse, the marriage partner began to show signs of disturbance. Later on it was found that when a schizophrenic youngster was removed from his family and hospitalized, another sibling frequently began to show psychotic disturbances. These observations can probably be explained by gestalt psychology—people with dormant difficulties gain strength and a self-image of health in comparing themselves with a family member who is obviously sick. It was even more dynamically explained by Nathan W. Ackerman in his famous scapegoat theory[10] in which he suggested that the designated child patient of a family was in reality the recipient of the projections of pathology of other family members and apparently an obedient respondent to the expectations resulting from these projections. At any rate, it seemed to be indicated that if one wanted to help a family member in trouble, one would have to help all

*See also Chapter 1, p. 13.

family members to experience changes which would make it unnecessary for them to keep the designated patient in his impairment.

Other therapists such as Don Jackson and Virginia Satir[11] concurred with the communication theory of Gregory Bateson[12] and emphasized for the explanation of family difficulties the theory of the "double bind."* This is essentially a miscommunication theory which explains behavioral difficulties by the reception of contradictory signals. A mother may, for instance, take her child on her lap and say words of love to the child while the rigidity of her body sends a message to him that the mother does not like his physical closeness and, thus, does not like him. The communication may also be faulty in that it gives an inhibition but does not indicate the desirable alternative of behavior.

A third important theory underlying family treatment is the one developed by Murray Bowen,[13] who bases his explanation and therapeutic effort on the theory of the disturbing existence of an undifferentiated family ego mass, a term which he later discarded. In such family constellations every family member experiences what is happening to others as happening to him and therefore increases experientially his difficulties by taking upon himself the difficulties of the total family membership. The one least able to differentiate himself risks becoming psychotic.

Every one of the theories mentioned above suggests, of course, a different type of therapeutic goal. With Ackerman it is the liberation of the "scapegoat," with Jackson and Satir the clarification of communication and with Murray Bowen the increase of the individuation of the family members.

The technique in all the cases is the holding of therapeutic sessions with the total family membership, although of course infants and sometimes children who are too unruly, or have inadequate mental development, are excluded. During the therapeutic session relationships between family members are not reported to the therapist but demonstrated to him in action. There is no "aboutism" in the therapeutic process. The reality of family life is experienced with the therapist becoming a member of the family system which thereby changes from a rigid and hurtful one into one that is developing and therapeutic. The family members begin to listen where they formerly have been only talking and, for the most part, to themselves. They identify with the therapist and begin to play the role of co-diagnosticians and co-therapists for the other family mem-

*See also Chapter 2, p. 17.

bers. They discover that family secrets can be revealed and family relationships restructured with relaxation of the prohibitions they may have had in this regard.

The multiplicities of interactions which these therapeutic methods present to the therapist tax him with the demand for incessant and comprehensive observation. Family therapists are anxious that they will miss clues and are reassured by the presence of a co-therapist on whom they think they can rely—rightly or wrongly—so he will catch what they have missed. Whether valid or not, this furnishes a measure of relaxation to the co-therapist, who takes an active part in the group process. Co-therapists of different sex also present models of mature spouse relationships which, of course, run the risk of giving rise to the concommitant feelings of the therapists toward one another which thus requires sorting out after the session. Co-therapists of course will have to be aware that they represent a stimulus to family members, to manipulate them, to make them take opposite sides, and to bring them into conflict with one another.

REFERENCES

1. J. H. Pratt, "The Class Method of Treating Consumption in the Home of the Poor," *Journal of the American Medical Association,* August 31, 1907; "Results Obtained in the Treatment of Pulmonary Tuberculosis by the Class Method," *British Medical Journal,* October 10, 1908.
2. H. I. Harris "Efficient Psychotherapy for the Large Outpatient Clinic," *New England Journal of Medicine,* July, 1939.
3. R. W. Buck, "Class Method in Treatment of Essential Hypertension," *Annals of Internal Medicine,* September, 1937.
4. M. N. Chappell, J. J. Stefano, J. S. Rogerson, and F. H. Pike, "Value of Group Psychological Procedures in Treatment of Peptic Ulcers," *American Journal of Digestive Diseases and Nutrition,* January, 1937.
5. Paul Schilder, "The Analysis of Ideologies as a Psychotherapeutic Method, Especially in Group Treatment," *American Journal of Psychiatry,* November, 1936.
6. Louis Wender, "Dynamics of Group Psychotherapy and Its Application," *Journal of Nervous and Mental Diseases,* July, 1936; "Group Psychotherapy, A Study of Its Application," *Psychiatric Quarterly,* October, 1940; "Group Psychotherapy within the Psychiatric

Hospital," in *Current Therapies of Personality Disorders,* ed. Bernard Glueck, New York, Grune and Stratton, Inc., 1946.

7. S. R. Slavson, *Analytic Group Psychotherapy with Children, Adolescents and Adults,* New York, Columbia University Press, 1950; S. R. Slavson, ed. *The Practice of Group Therapy,* New York, International Universities Press, 1947.

8. Mildred Burgum, "The Father Gets Worse: A Child Guidance Problem", *American Journal of Orthopsychiatry,* XII, (July 1942) p. 474.

9. Bela Mittelmann, "Complementary Neurotic Reactions in Intimate Relationships," *Psychoanalytic Quarterly,* vol. 13, October, 1944, pp. 482-483.

10. Nathan W. Ackerman, *The Psychodynamics of Family Life,* New York, Basic Books, Inc., 1958.

11. Don D. Jackson and Virginia M. Satir, "Family Diagnosis and Family Therapy" in *Exploring the Bases for Family Therapy,* N. Ackerman, F. L. Beatman and S. N. Sherman, eds., New York, Family Service Association, 1961, pp. 29-51.

12. Gregory Bateson, *Steps to an Ecology of Mind,* New York, Ballantine Books, Inc., Chandler Publishing Company, 1972.

13. Murray Bowen, "The Family as the Unit of Study and Treatment"; Family Psychotherapy, Workshop, 1959, *American Journal of Orthopsychiatry,* Vol. 31: pp. 40-60, 1961; "A Family Concept of Schizophrenia", in *Etiology of Schizophrenia,* D. D. Jackson, ed., New York Basic Books, Inc., 1960, pp. 346-372.

CHAPTER IX

A SHARED DESTINY BETWEEN HELPER AND CLIENT OR PATIENT— NECESSITY OR NOT

Largely as a consequence of the self-assertion of women and Black people in relation to social change, medicine and social work have been frequently confronted with the demands that belonging to the same population group determines the appropriateness of a constellation between professional helper and client or patient. Members of the Woman's Movement demand the services of female gynecologists, and Black social workers claim special competence in servicing Black clients. The intensity of social revolution conceals the fact that the helping professions have expressed similar principles in the past. Psychoanalysts have been required to undergo the experience of analysis; social work students, particularly in the Pennsylvania School of Social Work, have been required to expose themselves to painful experiences in order to acquire an understanding of how a client feels.

It has also been observed that occasionally some outstanding dermatologists and specialists in pulmonary diseases have in their youth suffered the afflictions treated in their specialties. The underlying principle in all of these observations seems to be sound. It expresses the recognition that distance of experience between physician, psychologist and social worker on the one hand and patient or client on the other can be an obstacle to therapy. In practical application, however, this principle has potentially undesirable consequences and ultimately leads to absurdity. It islands and segregates helpers and clients, and it confines the helper within the limits of his personal or group experience. Furthermore, this principle cannot be extended to all types of clients and patients. It would, for instance, imply that only retired professionals could serve retired people and that only physicians with terminal illness could treat patients with terminal illness.

The essential problem of professional education is, therefore, the development of an ability to decrease the barrier of difference between physician and patient and social worker and client without making this decrease dependent upon belongingness to the same demographic category. One result of professional training must be to enable a younger person to empathize with an older person, a woman to help a male client, a male physician to help a woman patient, a Black professional to help a white client or patient, and vice-versa. One problem of training is, therefore, to develop the ability to gain out of one's own experience an understanding of somebody with another experience and to convey this understanding in such a way to the client or patient that he feels not only understood but also respected in his difference.

Between women and men this does not seem to present an insuperable difficulty. The principle of bisexuality[1,2] presents the starting point for such understanding and decrease of difference. Since every human being contains in his biological endowment the potential of femaleness as well as maleness which only under hormonal influence makes the characteristics of one or the other sex predominant, it is not inconceivable for a male professional helper to draw on his dormant femininity and have a female helper to draw on her dormant masculinity to understand the experience of belonging to the other sex. The obstacle to overcome is primarily the wish for unity[3] and for a conflict-free biological destiny which makes people reluctant to recognize the suppressed bisexual component in themselves. These strivings, of course, are or until recently have been socially supported. Boys with female character traits have been derided as "sissies," girls with male charactertraits as "tomboys" and, on the adult level, women reproached for masculinity and men for femininity. With the exchangeability of life tasks between males and females in our times, these social props are fast disappearing, and efforts to understand in one's own experience the experience of the other sex will not be so obstructed. However, there will remain residues of experience—the menstrual cycle in women and erection in males—which people will not be able to dredge out of their own potential of experience. There the distance of difference must be decreased by the giving and receiving of information. Men will have to be taught by women what psychological experiences accompany menstruation, pregnancy and menopause and, possibly, frigidity. Men will have to teach women what experiences precede, accompany and follow erection or impotence, and both will have to be taught how either sex experiences the other in terms of love and hate. In that respect the Women's Movement and consciousness-raising with its expression of long-accumulated anger against men would provide a very important resource of information for male helpers in their relationship to women patients or clients. For the time being no similar outlet of hostility of males for females can be put into the service of women professionals who treat men. In the 1930's the mother of the famous sociologist Paul F. Lazarsfeld, Sophie Lazarsfeld, wrote a book in German entitled *Wie Die Frau Den Mann Erlebt,* which tells essentially how a woman experiences men.[4] A similar book on how a man experiences women should be written. Ultimately four areas of experience should be made accessible to male and female professionals alike: How woman experiences being woman, how women experience their encounters with men, how man experiences being man, and how men experience their encounters with women.

For a young person to help an old client or patient represents similar difficulties and similar opportunities of overcoming these difficulties. The problem seems to lie primarily in the fact that young people and probably people well into their middle years are under the spell of the dramatic growth and maturation experienced during their first twenty years of life. Although physical growth comes to an end at roughly that time, social development seemingly continues the experience. Increasing professional stature, increasing income, the experience of marriage and paranthood, the widening web of relation ships and experiences suggests a continuation of growth which conceals the fact that physiological decline may be well on the way. This can be dredged out of one's experience in the service of professional competence and decreasing distance from older patients and clients. The change in the firmness of her breasts and the general decline of tissue elasticity which we connect with the concept of female beauty can be used by every woman professional as a path to the understanding of the impact on the self-image of a deteriorating body of an aging person. The decline in the capacity to run could do the same for men in the professions. We only blind ourselves to physiological decline in the 20's and 30's because our self-perception still operates under the law of good continuation and is not forced into correction by the impact of dramatic structural change. This, however, is a privilege of ignorance which should be denied to professional persons. The principle of recognition of decline in one's body and impairment of the self-image should not be foreign to the professional person and will lead him to empathize with persons who are further along the road of such development.

Again, information from older persons about experiences of aging should be made available to the physicians and social workers in training. The strange phenomenon of "aboutism" is rampant in the literature of social gerontology: in most publications younger people talk "about" older people or report the answers of older persons to questions which younger persons have formulated. There is relatively little direct information expressed spontaneously by the aged. The aged are, therefore, compelled to confirm or to deny the preconceptions of the young about aging. It is interesting to note that in the *Handbook of Aging and the Individual*,[5] the phenomenon of fatigue is only mentioned on one page and only in relation to pupil fatigue. The global phenomenon of fatigue as a concurrent experience of being aged seems to have escaped all the major writers in the field. Similarly, one of the gratifications regularly available to aged people, namely, physical recuperation, understood in its elational sense, does not seem to have reached the awareness of the specialists in the field of social gerontology. However, it should not be impossible to correct this lack of information in the curricula of schools of medicine and social work because more and more professional people concerned with aging are currently experiencing the phenomenon of getting older and being old. There is reason for optimism that their concern and specialization will soon turn into experiential expertise and furnish the information so long obstructed by youthful projection so that it can reach younger persons at that point. Based on the experience of the writer, a number of essential phenomena should be conveyed to physicians and social workers. First of all is the principle of constancy of personality. Active people remain active, passive people remain passive, loving people remain loving, and aggressive people remain aggressive over the life span. It is therefore likely to be erroneous to ascribe personality characteristics to age-change short of strokes and senility. The monotony of human motivation is likely to permit the professional helper to make a prediction of behavior of the aged person in the foreseeable future. In spite of this constancy of individuation, the universality of the experience of decline and the stimulation of death anxieties has to become part of the evaluation of the coping problems of an older patient or client. The angry reaction to the experience of relative weakness, loss of sensory capacities, social devaluation and threat of nothingness can probably be made understandable to a younger person by reference to his own experience of anger in the experience of failure or relative inferiority. It is equally important to convey the compensations. A wise psychoanalyst, Robert Waelder, once said to the author that every level of comfort has its own discomfort. It should be proposed that the reverse statement is also true and that every level of discomfort has its own comfort. The pervasive fatigue of old age has its special comfort of repetitive recuperation and rest. Insomnia has the comfort of not being bombarded at night by sensory stimuli which the decline of sensory capacities makes burdensome during the daytime hours of the aged. The loss of friends and relatives also presents an experience of liberation and of being set free for other options. Although these options may become fewer with advancing years, they certainly become more accessible than they were before the loss or bereavement occurred. There is, therefore, existential comfort in loss which old people are frequently ashamed to admit and, when they do, are being censured for it. Ultimately the ambivalence toward one's own aging self makes mortality acceptable. People get fed up with being sick and old, with being in pain, afraid of dying. It is very likely that most people at one stage or another change the will to live into the will to die and that a humane professional would perceive this wish and not obstruct it or fight it with the equipment of modern medical instrumentation. It is again the projection of the young person who irrationally believes in his own immortality to assume that old people at no point in time want to die.

On the other hand, older persons frequently make it very difficult for younger persons to be helpful to them and to empathize with them. The hostility aroused by one's own decline, the irritability of repetitive experiences of deficits in seeing, hearing, walking and sleeping turns the old against the young. It seduces them into using their own suffering as a weapon against the young, to use their own discomforts and feelings to frighten their younger associates and to create thereby a loneliness around themselves which spells ultimate suffering and despair. Anyone who goes through a ward of medicine or surgery in a general hospital will find emptiness around the beds or in the rooms of the aged patients. One gains the impression that they drive relatives, nurses, and physicians away by presenting a hostile and frightening presence. To be "old and alone" is only partly the result of natural law or the result of social disengagement. It is often selfmade by people who have not learned conduct-norms appropriate to old age. The exchange principle works on all levels of human development. Old people will have to learn from the young what they can give to them and young people will have to learn from the old what the old person needs in exchange. One may suggest that what the old can give to the young is to set them free from the psychological tie to parental figures so that they do not have to connect the experience of their loss as destruction of self. Furthermore, the old can furnish illustration of the attainment of wholeness in the completion of one's life tasks and the experience of nonlimiting care. Old people care for the young but they do so mostly in a parental, directive and age-inappropriate fashion. This age inappropriateness relates both to the actual stage of development of the young as well as the relevance of the experience of the old. What appears to be a young person to an old person is likely to be an adult. On the other hand, the self-image of adulthood of an old person is probably obsolete. He is not anymore an adult, he does not fully understand what it means to be an adult. In simple terms, young people and older people may live at the same time, but they are not contemporaries.

In closing, professionals more than other people need humility when confronted with difference. There will always be ultimate barriers to understanding between different people. It is a temptation and a pitfall of professional training to assume that one must know everything about the person to be helped and that there is nothing that cannot be known. Professionals are trained to uncover causes or rather to believe that they can. This, in confrontation with difference, is a grave relationship risk. When the social worker or physician conveys to the client or patient the impression that he is not only ignorant but also ignorant of his ignorances, the element of trust in the helping process will be irremediably impaired.

REFERENCES

1. Marie Bonaparte, *Female Sexuality,* New York, Grove Press Inc., 1965, pp. 11-16.
2. Mary Jane Sherfey, *The Nature and Evolution of Female Sexuality,* New York, Random House, Inc., 1972, pp. 30-53.
3. Gustav Ichheiser, "Misunderstandings in Human Relations," *American Journal of Sociology,* Vol. LV, No. 2 (Sept. 1949), pp. 27-31.
4. Sophie Lazarsfeld, *Woman's Experience of the Male,* London, Aldor, 1940, Hackensack, Wehman Bros., 1974.
5. *Handbook of Aging and the Individual,* James E. Birren, ed., University of Chicago Press, 1959, p. 508.

CHAPTER X

OVERCOMING
OF DIFFERENCES—
RACIAL AND ETHNIC

The encounter of a physician, nurse or social worker with a patient or client who presents a different racial or ethnic background has also been considered as presenting problems of distance which prevent full understanding. Such differences are usually seen only from the viewpoint of obstacles to the helping process and have frequently led to the establishment of organizations designed to service specific population groups. Jewish hospitals, Catholic hospitals, Catholic charities, Urban Leagues, HIAS, and Jewish family services have long been part of the American helping scene. Although they have always been justified in terms of meeting the special needs of the patients or clients, cynics have frequently suggested that they are really serving the professionals of a specific religious, ethnic or racial background by providing employment free from the handicap of discrimination and by monopolizing certain patient and client groups. In more recent times these segregated service arrangements have also been formed in connection with social movements, such as the Black revolution and the Women's Movement.

However, the geographical and social mobility operating in the United States makes these segregated institutional arrangements very vulnerable to changing conditions. Jewish hospitals find themselves stranded in neighborhoods that have become Italian or Black, as happened in

Philadelphia. German institutions, such as Lankenau Hospital, find themselves in suburban locations where there are few Germans left. Even synagogues find themselves in Black neighborhoods as Jewish members of the originally lower socioeconomic status, will leave the neighborhood when they attain better economic conditions, and other non-Jewish people will move in. It will, therefore, be part and parcel of the American scene that helper and client or patient will have to cope with the problem of cultural, racial or religious differences.

One of the most obvious forms of overcoming these difficulties is an attempt to convey information to the professional helper suggesting that knowledge about the subculture of the client will facilitate the helping process. Sometimes this information is conveyed by books such as *Life is with People: The Jewish Little Town of Eastern Europe* by Mark Zborowski and Elizabeth Herzog;[1] *The Irish Countryman* by Conrad Arensberg;[2] *The Chrysanthemum and the Sword* by Ruth Benedict;[3] *The Negro Family in the U.S.* by E. Franklin Frazier;[4] or more recent books like *Black Rage* by Wm. H. Grier and Price M. Cobbs;[5] and *Black Families in White America* by Andrew Billingsley.[6] Although these books give information which people not belonging to the specific population group may find useful by furnishing some explanations of behavior or emotion by which the professional helper may have been puzzled or of which he may have been unaware, these sources of information have never really been integrated into the theories or techniques of helping. In the following pages an attempt will be made to respond to the challenge of this condition. First of all, one must realize that the client or patient is probably a better source of pertinent information about his cultural, racial or religious specificity than any book because it represents his personalized perception of his subculture rather than the perception of a scholar or researcher. It also may be more up-to-date—or more obsolete—than publications available in this respect. It may therefore be helpful in the encounter between professional helper and client to tap this source of information as part of the exchange between the two as early as possible in the contact. This must be done carefully, however, as it may run against traditional apprehensions of minority people about revealing their life fully to a member of a dominant group. A member of the helping profession will give the appearance of dominance not only because of his own cultural, racial or religious specificity, but also because of his position of superiority in the helping process. It is very likely that Jewish patients will not tell a gentile physician or a gentile nurse about their feelings of apprehension regarding anti-Semitism. It is very likely that Black clients will withhold from white social workers information about their way of life, not only because of their expectation of disapproval but also because their hostility will find gratification in withholding information that the physician or social worker wants to know. The professional helper finds himself, therefore, in a dilemma. If he goes to books, they may not reflect the experience of the individual and if he goes to the client or patient, he may encounter withholding.

The answer seems to lie not so much in finding out more than one knows but in learning to help with what is available either in the literature or in the information offered by the client. This suggestion violates one of the most cherished beliefs of American civilization, namely, that an increase of information facilitates the decision-making process. As a matter of fact, it might be proposed that the opposite is true—that an increase of information complicates decision-making. One might suggest that humility, *vis-a-vis* the unknown specificity of the client or patient, may be a more viable principle of helping and actually be strengthening to the client by leaving him an area of privacy which the helping process will not touch. This applies to all areas of interviewing which are essentially invasive and, as such, potentially offensive. An area in which such moderation in the quest for information is not desirable, however, is the realm of reactions to the encounter with strangeness within the professional helper. Is he blinding himself against the fact that he may be hated by the client because of his color, religion, or socioeconomic status? Does he have a need to be loved where cooperation would be sufficient, even if it were antagonistic cooperation? Does one not have antagonisms toward specific client or patient groups which lead one to shorten an interview and choose to rely on stereotype information rather than seeking case-appropriate understanding? Does one have a reaction formation in which one denies, for instance, one's sexism or racism to the point of projecting the client's difficulties upon society in cases in which personal problems furnish a more parsimonious explanation and offer a hope of helping which does not have to wait for social change? Is it not possible that a female client may have a career problem based on her personality and not on her sex or that a Jewish client may have a problem not rooted in the relationship with his mother? It is an old experience that we avert our eyes from people whom we dislike. Helping this averting of eyes can simply be done by putting stereotypes—old and new—in the place of case specific understanding. I would propose that the problems of Blackness in the helping process are as much, if not more so, the problems of the white worker with blackness than the problems of the Black client with the white society. In spite of these reservations, however, it should not be forgotten that culture, in the experience of a person, is largely coping with the difficulties that are created by traditional ways of life. Since all cultures present problems in intracultural as well as intercultural contacts, a cultural inheritance usually contains a message of the desirability of change. At the same time, it contains a message of maintenance of identity. This is probably well illustrated by married Jewish women who keep a Kosher household but refuse to wear a wig *(Shitel)*. The same occurs probably in the wish of Black people to fight discrimination and, at the same time, to separate themselves from the integration proposals of white liberals. It expresses itself in the birth control practices of the Catholic who still goes to confession, and in all advocacy-strivings of minority group members who accept positions in the establishment. Even leadership of protest groups represents such an ambivalent coping with a double bind of cultural inheritance and the wish to overcome minority status. One must assume, therefore, that in most clients and patients from minority groups in the United States, there is ambivalence between the wish to retain cultural identity and the wish to join the dominant group, especially as it offers access to its resources. It would seem, therefore, to be a problem of goal-setting to help the patient or client to overcome this ambivalence so that he can realize that there are no "bargains"—one must pay a price for what one decides to do. In this instance, this means that one can maintain cultural specificity only at the price of exposure to hostility and that one can only attain equal access to resources by giving up one's subcultural identity.

Hidden behind all this decision-making is the wish of choosing between the quality and quantity of life. It has been one of the largely disregarded results of medical advancement that people are increasingly deprived of the foods that they want. Fats, starches, or sugar may be forbidden for sound medical reasons. Since food intake is a primary process connected with the idea of receiving love, however, one might wonder whether physicians know what they have to offer in lieu of these deprivations which they prescribe. The likelihood that one will die of cancer rather than of a coronary occlusion, that one will get crippling arthritis before one dies, that one will lose increasingly one's hearing, sight, one's friends, spouses and siblings offer very small inducements to undergo such deprivations, if any. What is it that medicine has to offer in lieu of primary gratification? This is a special problem for such ethnic groups as Blacks, Jews and Italians, where food has long been the compensation for deprivation.

Similarly, one must ask the questions, "What am I really asking from people if I insist on good sanitation and cleanliness?" as white middle-class people in the professions do. First of all cleanliness is hard work; to clean one's house is extra effort; to keep it clean is endless effort; to keep it clean when one has a large number of children is impossible. How many doctors or public health nurses balance the comfort of a dog against the health benefits of cleanliness? For children dogs are amiable companions who do not treat the child as a nuisance (as many adults will), who do not tire of the child's company, but most of all who do not set limits. To an old person a dog is largely a nonrejecting companion, an organism to be taken care of; in other words, a giver of meaning to a life which may appear to have become meaningless.

In summary, I would suggest that cultural, racial and religious differences should not be overstated in their importance for the helping process. The helping process, like all other forms of human strategy, must be assumed to work between people who are willing either in the beginning or in the development of their relationship to provide one another with information needed for the task. More specifically, it must be assumed that a professional person can be trained to know his own resistance to receiving information and to respect the resistance of the client to giving information. The helping process must also work with the assumption that patients will have enough sanity to accept help from somebody who does not fully understand them, and it must be assumed that such work is possible. Financial assistance, grudgingly and punitively given, will still buy food. Surgery performed by a white hand on a black body must still be assumed to be professionally performed. Marital problems of Italians may still be accessible to counseling by Jewish psychiatrists, and so on. Limitations of human understanding and the existence of human antagonism must not be considered as incompatible with helping since a measure of sanity and the professional demand of self-knowledge can be assumed to operate and to be safeguarded by professional standards and common sense on both sides of the helping process. It is perhaps in this dimension that supervision and consultation with professional peers who share race and ethnicity with the client and professional experiences over time can be most helpful.

REFERENCES

1. Mark Zborowski and Elizabeth Herzog, *Life is with People: The Jewish Little Town of Eastern Europe,* New York, International Universities Press, 1952.
2. Conrad M. Arensberg, *The Irish Countryman,* New York, MacMillan, Inc., 1937.
3. Ruth Fulton Benedict, *The Chrysanthemum and the Sword,* Boston, Houghton Mifflin, 1946.
4. E. Franklin Frazier, *The Negro Family in the United States,* Chicago, University of Chicago Press, revised and abridged, 1966.
5. William H. Grier and Price M. Cobbs, *Black Rage,* New York, Basic Books, Inc., 1968.
6. Andrew Billingsley, *Black Families in White America,* Englewood Cliffs, N. J., Prentice-Hall, 1968.

CHAPTER XI

OVERCOMING OF DIFFERENCES— FAMILIAL

In the field of family counseling in particular, differences in familial experiences between counselor and client can occur on developmental, structural, functional and dysfunctional ground. It is a common occurrence that the woman client who has children will question the competence and empathy of a social worker who has none. Even if this question is not verbalized, it will be in the client's mind and often in the therapist's. This will tend to interfere with the relationship. The answer could lie in the fact that, although the worker has no children, he or she has been a child. On the other hand there may be familial differences between client and worker which cannot be so easily overcome. It may be impossible for a person who has not experienced divorce to use the developmental argument or a person who is not widowed to overcome the argument that anybody who has not suffered such bereavement cannot empathize fully with the experience of definite separation. It may be equally difficult for a worker who has been an only child to imagine what it means to grow up with ten siblings in the house.

The situation is not hopeless if the worker has enough powers of abstraction and sense of generalization to find commonality between his or her experience and the experience of the client. Every person in the United States, whether an only child or not, has had a generalized experience of having quasi-sibling relationships in the school setting. He or She will have experienced scarcity in attention from a teacher which a person with many siblings in all likelihood will have experienced from a parent. A person who has not known divorce has had to learn separation from parents, from siblings, from lovers and, thus, should be able to abstract out from his own experience the experience of loss, self-questioning, need for replacement, and sorrow that a divorced person feels.

The principle to apply here is to abstract out of one's own life experience either by way of recall or by way of generalized commonality—common factors which are applicable to the concreteness of the problems of the client.

On a more theoretical level, empathy for a familial experience can probably be derived from the conceptual framework of C. G. Jung's *Two Essays on Analytical Psychology*.[1] To understand and to use this material, it is important to keep in mind that the difference between Freudian psychoanalytical thinking and Jungian analytical psychology lies essentially in the content of unconscious material as perceived by the analyst. For Freud the unconscious material was limited by the life history of the patient, by experience which could not be started before birth, and which was essentially idiosyncratic. Jung observed that in the unconscious of his patients there seemed to be universal recurrent themes such as the concept of wholeness, the concept of opposites and the concept of universal parental figures. Finding these represented in the mythology of primitive people, he called them archtypes.

Of course one must question whether such phenomena can really be confined to the unconscious—their existence and relevance is obviously part of the conscious of most people. In order to derive benefit from the concept of the archtypes, one must assume that they represent a threat to human beings because they suggest a deficit in one's own life and personality, present a challenge of the unattainable and ultimately force the human being into a confrontation with what he is not and feels he should be. The concept of wholeness suggests to human beings that they are only parts of the human condition—male or female, introverts or extroverts, fathers or mothers. This confrontation is stimulated by the primary bisexuality of the individual who under the convergence of physiological maturation and socialization is being forced into becoming a specialized part of the general human condition. On the conscious level one feels bisexuality to be a threat while on the unconscious level sexual identity may be the stimulus of anxiety. The chest structure of a male is, of course, the potential of breast development which is frequently experienced as a threat by aging persons who, under glandular dysfunction, notice body changes which they have been conditioned to associate with the specificity of the female body. The glandular changes in the female body may produce hair on the face of women which they have learned to identify as a male characteristic. On the conscious level, therefore, human beings have been conditioned to identify themselves as belonging to one or the other sex, and they become anxious when this stereotype of sexual specificity seems to be disturbed. On the unconscious level, however, specificity may mean incompleteness, separation from the wholeness of the human condition, a need for completion through someone else who is different and conceivably hostile. It implies the risk of dependency on someone unlike oneself and is, therefore, threatening.

Familial life can be seen from that vantage point as an unconsciously determined attempt to establish wholeness through union. This experience is most significantly achieved in heterosexual intercourse and is being sought after repeatedly. Here, however, we come up against a paradox. Compared with the amount of time that people spend in striving for heterosexual union, thinking about it, looking for a partner, motivating the intended partner to engage in the experience, the actual amount of time during which the union is so achieved is absurdly small. The attempt of a female and a male to achieve wholeness through heterosexual intercourse is therefore to be seen as a long time, if not a lifetime preoccupation, with only ephemeral moments of attainment.

A closer approach to permanence of the experience of wholeness seems to result from conception. It is only in the fusion of egg and sperm resulting in a child that the wholeness striving of male and female seems to promise any lasting fulfillment. Here, however, the human striving for wholeness gets into trouble almost from the start. A child is separated from his mother by the act of birth, and in the process of maturation and development, he is separated from his parents. When a mother cannot bring herself to permit and even facilitate the separation, we have severe developmental problems which have been conceptualized as symbiotic relationships, noted by M. S. Mahler in "Child Psychosis and Schizophrenia, Autistic and Symbiotic Infantile Psychoses" and "Symbiotic Child Psychosis: Genetic Dynamic and Restitutive Aspects."[2] To make matters worse the sex of the child represents to the parents the ultimate unattainability of wholeness in the human condition. If one's own sex implies separation and fractionalization of wholeness, then the sex of the child repeats one's own destiny of separation. This is probably the reason why people prefer to have children of both sexes and sometimes engage in a greater number of reproductive attempts than they would if they had children of both sexes. Everyone knows the pathetic humor of a couple with five girls or five boys who, close to the climacteric, engage in another conception and produce once more a child of the same sex. Having, almost in desperation, wanted to add a sister to their five boys, they end up with six boys.

In this conceptual framework of understanding, differences of familial experience between the professional helper and the person to be helped dwindle into insignificance. The familial experiences of *all* people become understandable as a striving for wholeness, for union attempted, for union experienced as ephemeral, and for union doomed to end in spearation. The goal of helping thus becomes the acceptance of individuation by the client whether he has ten siblings or none, has children or is childless, has been divorced or is unmarried, is Black or white, Irish or Jewish, old or young.

It is thus abstraction of the commonality of the problems of separation and individuation which enables a psychiatrist or other therapist to bridge the apparent gulf of differences in familial experience. It also represents a mental health goal which is not only acceptance but ultimately the enjoyment of the human condition of separation. This then makes striving for wholeness an attempt of undoing or denying rather than a search for fullfillment.

Related questions of probably universal application are whether mothers are more closely related to children than fathers and whether childless marriages are not more conducive to peace of mind than marriages with children. Again the dimension of time in relation to experience has to be considered. A pregnancy of nine months may produce for many women an experience of relatedness to the child as a symbol of having attained wholeness which, in comparison with the man's part in reproduction, appears to be overwhelming. The fetus can truly be seen as belonging to the mother, and she carries the attainment of wholeness in her body. It is conceivable of course that on the conscious level the fetus may be experienced as an intruder, as a perpetual reminder of an invasion of the mother's body, but it is also possible that the negative feelings about the fetus as an invader are on the unconscious level, a flight from a wholeness which an individual may not dare to admit. Whether experienced as an invader or experienced as a fulfillment of wholeness, the fetus in uninterrupted pregnancy literally ties mother and child together as no father and child can ever be tied. It may be an unwelcome tie, but the noun is still *tie.* If, in the course of medical advance, it should become possible to grow fertilized human eggs in cultures rather than in a mother's body, this special tie between mother and child may disappear from the human experience. The attainment of this condition, however, is not likely to become universal in the foreseeable future. It should also be considered that the father's physiological disability to establish similar ties with his children may produce a type of envy associated with feelings of physiological inferiority. What is the size of a seed compared with the dimension of the enveloping soil? That feelings of inferiority may lead to reaction-formation and together with pretechnological cultural conditions may produce patriarchal family systems need not surprise.

It has been frequently found that childless marriages seem to be less troubled than marriages in which the spouses have produced children. A cynic could, of course, say that since human beings are trouble, the more human beings you find in the family, the more troubles there will be. One could go further, however, and realize that despite his symbolic value of wholeness, the child during the process of separation from his parents permanently stimulates the parents' anxiety about not being whole. The more children, the more separations, the more stimuli of the return of unconscious anxiety about not being whole into the consciousness of the parent.

This conceptual framework of the universality of familial experience is, of course, not presented here as supported by clinical evidence but is experientially based and can probably be so validated by many readers. It should be kept in mind as an example of ways of overcoming the distance between professional helper and client or patient based on familial differences. The principle underlying this, as stated earlier, is based on the process of abstraction from the helper's concrete experiences leading to the recognition of commonality which permits the application of that experience to the concreteness of experience of the client.

This principle, however, may not help in overcoming differences in familial experiences resulting either in neurotic disabilities or in depressions. Between the neurotic person and the depressed person, it is difficult to visualize a level of abstraction which would permit an understanding of the other. The neurotic is essentially an optimist who has found in his disability a method of anxiety-reduction which, in itself, represents a success in coping, albeit one which is distrubing and maladaptive. The depressed person is essentially a pessimist, a person who has been unsuccessful in coping and because he can no longer deny his inadequacy, attempts to use exploitation of others or aggression against them. He has failed in his attempts to reduce his anxieties and, in consequence, has recurrent periods of hopelessness. Optimism resulting from coping colors the attitude of the neurotic toward himself. He is not only optimistic about tension reduction, he is also optimistic about receiving help with his disability. The depressed person has no such optimism about himself or the helping process. There arises then the question whether a neurotic psychiatrist or social worker can help a depressed person or, even more devastatingly, the question whether a depressed person can help a depressed person. The neurotic will not understand, and the depressed professional helper will lack the confidence which one must have in one's helping powers. In such situations one must fall back on crisis treatment which is always treatment of people who are afraid of hopelessness. A person in crisis is ultimately pessimistic about the outcome of an experience of traumatic change. What one can do for such a person in essentially to be existentially there until the change resolves itself into a manageable situation. In essence, this amounts to providing company to a lonely person in temporary distress. In such situations the differences in experience between the helper and the person to be helped cannot be overcome but need not be overcome. What the helper can do is relieve the experience of loneliness of the client or patient until conditions change and coping appears to become possible. This method of helping, however, requires patience, defense against becoming irritated by an apparent lack of success, humility regarding one's own powers of intervention and, at best, being satisfied with contributing to survival. In more general terms, the difference in experience between psychiatrists and other therapists and their clients may lie in having overcome partially and for the most part problems the client finds difficult to overcome in any way or form. This may produce a special type of impatience and irritation in helpers who are unaware of the distance which this difference produces between them and their clients. Why can the client not stop smoking if I have stopped smoking? Why can he not stop using drugs if I have stopped using drugs? Why can he not break self-destructive patterns of behavior if I could do it? This irritation is essentially not an irritation with the client but an irritation with the self because fantasies about one's therapeutic powers have been frustrated. Why can I not help the client do what I could help myself to do is at the core of this feeling. It is the angry reaction to the helper's apprehension of professional inadequacy rather than the response to the stimulus provided by the obstinacy of the client.

It is probably one of the most disturbing experiences for members of the helping professions that professional training which should improve one's helping capacities by itself leads to difficulties in helping or at least creates obstacles which diminish the effectiveness of the helping potential one expects from such training. First among these is the feeling of superiority resulting from the acquisition of knowledge which the client or patient does not have. It is sometimes ironic to observe that psychiatrists and other therapists react negatively to the use of technical terms by clients or patients. This is often labelled as intellectualization, and many helpers seem to be unaware of the resentment which they feel about the clients' access to technological nomenclature. For organically-oriented physicians, a different problem often arises—namely, their inability to use language in explaining diseases and treatment procedures which a patient would understand. This finds sometimes dramatic expression in the informed consent forms which patients are asked to sign in relation to clinical research with human subjects. A third problem is the apparent difference between the professional helper and the client or patient in the evaluation of threatening terminology. To the anxious patient a Greek or Latin word may spell doom or at least danger. To the physician it may simply be the appropriate word for the patient's condition.

Professional training is also attitudinal. It tries to defend the helper against being overwhelmed by the pain and danger to which his patients are exposed. Technology may seem to fortify this defense, particularly for oncologists, but in effect it disturbs the potential relationship the patient craves in his anxiety and dependency. This is probably also a special defense of nurses on medical wards, particularly in intensive care units, and results in similar disturbances in the nurse-patient relationship.

REFERENCES

1. C. G. Jung, *Two Essays on Analytical Psychology,* New York, Bollingen Foundation, Inc., 1953; Princeton, N. J., Princeton University Press, 1972.
2. M. S. Mahler, "On Child Psychosis and Schizophrenia: Autistic and Symbiotic Infantile Psychoses," 1952, in *Psychoanalytic Study of the Child,* Vol. 7, pp. 286-305; "On Symbiotic Child Psychosis, Genetic dynamic and Restitutive Aspects," 1955, (same series) Vol. 10, pp. 195-212.

CHAPTER XII

THE HELPING BUREAUCRACIES AND PEOPLE IN CRISIS

Modern life involves itself and has to be experienced largely in the context of complex organizations. We are born in maternity wards of large hospitals. We spend a large part of our development until early adulthood in public or private school, colleges or universities. We seek employment with business or service organizations. We go for medical check-ups to physicians who rely on laboratories and test facilities for necessary information, and ultimately we die in hospitals.

Complex organizations are frequently called bureaucracies and are intricate attempts of making workable a division of labor and role distribution among large numbers of people. This implies an effort to minimize unpredictability in performance and to reduce human idiosyncrasies to ineffectiveness. In essence, it is an attempt to dehumanize the individual and to make him perform like a cog in a well-oiled machine. Max Weber[1] has identified the principles under which bureaucracies work as follows:

1. Bureaucracies operate on a continuous basis.
2. Every person in a bureaucracy performs his work in accordance with defined rules and without personal considerations and feelings.
3. Every person's responsibilities and authority are part of a hier-

archy so that supervision becomes in itself a function of all but the employees on the lowest level.

4. Officials do not own the resources of the organization.
5. Employment cannot be appropriated. i.e., it cannot be sold or inherited.
6. Business is conducted on the basis of written documents.

The last requirement gives an explanation of the term *bureaucracy*. The French word *bureau* means desk, the Greek word *crator* means ruler. A bureaucrat is, therefore, the ruler of the desk. This implies also one of the most significant burdens of physicians, social workers and nurses— namely, the writing of records which preserve what is being done for accountability, for supervision, and for the information of others who are cooperating in the process of the organization. Increasingly then, the desks become less places to write on than places to store what has been written. At the same time there is a feeling among many people in the organization that the recording takes away valuable time from other functions. It also offers a temptation of corruption, i.e., to report what should have been done rather than to report what has been done. One might even ask whether the notoriously bad handwriting of physicians is not due to the fact that they consider diagnosing and treating a more worthy performance of their professional task than writing on medical charts or writing prescriptions. With Medicare and, perhaps in the future, the National Health Service, there will be a temptation to delegate the writing to secretaries. Here we come up against a characteristic of bureaucracy which has not received sufficient attention—namely, the temptation to use the hierarchy for delegating unpleasant parts of one's own performance to somebody in a lower echelon. In a hospital, for instance, the line of delegation may go from Chief of Service to Staff Physician, to Staff Nurse, to Practical Nurse, to Student Nurse, to Aid. Lateral delegation may lead from physician to laboratory, X-ray Department, Occupational Therapy and Physical Therapy. Every delegation, however, means delay. The latter may be partly due to the time demanded for transfer of patient, blood samples or urine specimens from the office of the physician to the test installation and the return of the reports on these tests to the physician. It may also be due to the lack of coordination between two schedules, that of the physician and that of the laboratory; or to the antagonism which all hierarchical relationships contain. It was one of the monumental discoveries of industrial sociology to identify delays in performances not only as a result of complexity but as a result of informal organization which determines output and can keep it at a level lower than the potential of the work force.[2]

It must seem obvious by now that the nature of complex organization not only produces delays but also creates an essentially antagonistic work force. People do not like to be dehumanized, they resent supervision, and they object to the anxiety and possible injustices of accountability. It is a never-ceasing experience that many accountants or evaluators of service do not know the nature of the work which they have to examine and ultimately will evaluate it by criteria which are inappropriate and therefore unjust.

It is exceedingly difficult to expect people in a complex organization to perform their work without feelings, without love and hate, and, in the case of physicians, with affective neutrality.

It is perhaps the greatest contribution of social work to have developed a theory of helping which is based on relationship and thus in opposition to the impersonality postulated by the spirit of bureaucracy.

By and large, patients and clients manage to receive help from physicians, nurses and social workers in spite of the delay and nonresponsiveness of many persons employed in helping organizations. It might be useful to point out that the word *patient* is truly an appropriate term for sick people—if they wish to get help from the medical system, patience will be their most basic requirement. They must wait in waiting rooms. One cannot help but wonder why reception rooms should be called waiting rooms? Is being kept waiting a necessary part of the bureaucratic reception? Is being kept waiting in front of an X-ray laboratory, is being kept waiting for surgery until all the necessary tests have been made, is being kept waiting for an appointment sometimes until spontaneous recovery has occurred, an essential part of the medical service system? Part of it may well be unavoidable, part is obviously the result of an absence of the patient revolution which in sequence to the consumer revolution is very likely to come and thus bring about a vast number of changes.

Large numbers of people have learned not to claim medical services on holidays and weekends. Many psychiatric patients have learned to cope with their discomforts without psychiatric help in August when many psychiatrists go on vacation, and many people have learned to use the Emergency Room for nonemergencies because they refuse to be "patient patients." There is, however, one area in which the patience demanded in the medical service system may be a health threat and, thus, not only annoying but counterproductive. This is the waiting for test results in biopsies. In a society so beset with cancerophobia as ours, week-long delays in learning the test results produce such anxiety in many patients and their relatives, particularly spouses, parents and children, that one might wonder, from the point of view of public health, whether people with heart conditions or psychosomatic vulnerabilities do not suffer physical damage by the delays of the system. It defies the spirit of helping as well as that of simple humanity to create a crisis regularly under the banner of health maintenance and inflict anguish as well as potential health threat by prolonging the crisis and leaving the human subject unattended during the delay. There is no reason why one physician or a nurse cannot take a tissue sample, blood sample or specimen from a patient *and* make the test immediately, thus returning with the results while the patient is still in the office. There are signs that some practitioners have become aware of this and spare the patients the anguish of waiting as well as the risk of emotional and sometimes physical damage. It is to be hoped that their new approach will bring other practitioners in line; where this is not the case, pressure and public indignation will hopefully do the job. It should also be pointed out that it may be a function of medical social workers to keep in touch with patients who are waiting for test results and furnish supportive relationship during the crisis of waiting.

Another aspect of bureaucracy which interferes with the humanity, if not the effectiveness, of helping is the turnover of personnel. Rotation of interns and nurses, rotation of residents and, most of all, the mobility of social workers, make it frequently impossible for patients and clients to establish lasting relationships with physicians and other members of the helping professions in bureaucratic settings. The confidence built up by a positive encounter with a professional helper is, therefore, put in permanent jeopardy. It has to be established time and again; or it may well be withheld as a result of too many loss experiences. This change of personnel implies not only giving repeated case histories and loss of an established relationship, but also repetition of the diagnostic workup. A tremendous waste is involved in such conditions and, although the teaching process in the professions may make part of it unavoidable, part of it may well be eliminated by putting a premium on job constancy. It may also be desirable to make it part of professional training to dispel the expectation of greater happiness through changes of location or service. One could well visualize that physician, nurse and social worker employed in service organizations might be rewarded for job stability as well as for enhancement of their professional skills.

Perhaps the most important waste of time created by bureaucracy are the time demands of staff meetings, committee meetings, question-naires for internal and external use and the obstruction of scheduled activities by the never-ending impudence of deadline-making within complex organizations. Staff and committee meeting times are frequently an expression of sham democracy in which professional people are taken away from their work to be deluded into believing that they share in the decision-making of the organization to which they belong. Even where committee reports and staff resolutions involve decision-making, they are frequently based on the work of one or two persons who were more obstructed than helped by the other members of the body in accomplishing their task. Perhaps it is appropriate now to make a time-and-cost study of committee meetings in hospitals and social service organizations and to recast most of these time expenditures into time available for service.

Bureaucracy also creates the arrogance of setting deadlines. Everyone who wants a report or contribution or the payment of a bill for telephone service seems to feel entitled to set deadlines. These deadlines are always set without a thought to the work demands of the person who receives them. The convenience of the deadline-setter is claimed to be superior to the convenience of the person asked for the report, and certainly to be superior to the service demands of patients or clients. In summary, the urgency of the bureaucrat is always considered to be more urgent than the urgency of the service recipient.

It is not necessary to assume that bureaucracy is fortified against reform. Bureaucrats are essentially anxious people. Their anxiety may well be used for improvement of services if patients and clients insist on improvement of the system. Consumer unions are needed not only for the protection of buyers of physical merchandise, they are more needed for the protection from abuse or ill-use by medical and social service systems.

REFERENCES

1. Max Weber, *From Max Weber: Essays in Sociology,* New York Oxford University Press, 1947, pp. 196-244; *The Theory of Social and Economic Organization,* New York, Oxford University Press, 1947, pp. 329-341.
2. F. J. Roethlisberger and William J. Dickson, *Management and the Worker,* Cambridge, Harvard University Press, 1939; Peter M. Blau, *Bureaucracy in Modern Society,* New York, Random House, 1956.

CHAPTER XIII

TRENDS
OF
SOCIAL CHANGE

Any attempt to come to terms with universals in the helping experience must consider the phenomenon of social change as a problem for maintaining professional efficiency and as a problem of prediction, for the near future at least. Although helping directed at the individual has been accused of being conservative, it carries in itself the seeds of social change. All therapeutic goal-setting implies change. When people change, they are likely to affect the social arrangements under which they live. It is only a helping process which fails that is conservative in the strict sense of the terms. Psychoanalysis has been accused of being an outstanding example of such conservatism, but it has deeply affected child-rearing practices and the relationship of men and women to one another. It has done so directly through therapy but also indirectly through influencing government funding of research, parent education, literature and the mass media. Its impact on western civilization has been pervasive and has been helped even by publicity derived from heated scientific controversy. It has and is affecting the legal system, particularly in criminal law. It should, therefore, be stated that helpers are change agents by the nature of their work—even if the treatment goal of an individual were adjustment to the system, the system would be changed through the adjustment.

There is, however, a strong element of conservatism in the faithfullness of many professionals to the classics or what they perceive to be classics of their profession. Everybody who formulates a theory or developes a method of helping is likely to be time-bound in the data which he selects for attention and even more so by the data available at the time. There is, therefore, a strong tendency to maintain theory and practice without regard for changing data. It is the purpose of this chapter to bring to the attention of the reader a number of social changes which seem to require an adjustment in either theory or practice.

First of all, there is the growing impatience of people with waiting for the fulfillment of their expectations and with long term investments of energy or relationships in the pursuit of their goals. In the human sphere people seek instant gratification which makes every intervention that has a long-time perspective less desirable than a short-term perspective. Most of all, many clients and patients will now appear to be casualties of their claim for instant satisfaction. When people seek immediately gratifying relationships, they are bound to be disappointed with their partners. There will be then an ever-increasing temptation to change partner constellations rather than to improve the existing relationships. More and more clients and patients will appear to be two- and three-time losers. This will result in depressed clients suffering from a loss of hope rather than suffering from impairment in development and will lead to an increasing reliance on the impact of the body on the mind rather than on the impact of the mind on the body. The upsurge of sex therapies and the increasing use of psychotropic drugs are signs of this development.

Another group of casualties of social change will result from a clash of the facade of rebellion with the facade of nonresisting establishment. As a result of our scientific and political climate, many young people have been led to believe that rebellion is a career vehicle. Coming frequently from permissive homes and being supported by a theory of personality development which has presented the rebellion of adolescents as dynamically necessary and, therefore, as scientifically respectable, they have taken the apparently yielding reactions of governmental authorities, academic administrators and senior professionals at face value and have been shocked to learn that times spent in politics is time lost unless you are a politician. An assistant professor who has spent six years engaged in politics will find himself without scholastic record and, therefore, without tenure. Students who drop out of school to "find themselves" may find that the labor market has changed when they return to their studies. Young people who refused to fight and did not choose the exemptions available to conscientious objectors, may find that the establishment wants to take them back only on conditions unacceptable to the resisters.

In more generalized terms, the sheen of permissiveness which colors the reaction of parents, schools and even government in their reactions to the young, may frequently lead to rude awakenings or the impossibility of reentry when adolescence and early adulthood have passed and middle-age standards are applied to people led to believe that these standards had ceased to exist. Put in another way, our society increasingly has failed to signal youth that the permissiveness which youth encounters does not cover the life span.

With the increase in entrance of women into the professions and the labor market, the expectation of females to find fulfillment on the job will be exposed to reality-testing and will prove to many that in a complex society jobs are hardly sources of self-fulfillment. They may be remunerative and they may provide independence, but the utopian expectation of fulfillment is likely to be disappointed. Since the clock of time has never turned back, psychiatrists and marriage counselors as well as vocational counselors will probably have to cope with many cases of disappointment and needs for alternate strivings. The more our fight against discrimination of women and minorities will provide equal opportunity, the more will some people be faced with the task of coming to terms with experienced inferiority rather than with institutionally-assumed inferiority. The latter can always be accused as unjust and as an alibi of one's own failings. The former becomes a problem of self-image which will require a new type of ego-strength in coping. In cases in which the inferiority complex will be replaced by the inferiority experience, therapists will require new types of helping for members of population groups who have conquered discrimination. Perhaps even more interesting will be the impact of redistribution of child-rearing functions between parents and between home and childcare institutions. Different forms of regression, different stimuli of homosexuality and heterosexuality and different degrees of intensity in feelings and relationships are likely to result from these changes.

The helping professions may have to revise techniques designed to liberate patients and clients from the grip of the parent-child relationship which, because of their intensity and stability, had arrested development and led to impairments in adult life. They may have to develop treatment-goals and treatment-strategies which would help patients to overcome inabilities to form lasting relationships because they have had shallow emotional development.

In the relationship between population groups, we are soon likely to find in many white people a gratitude for not being hated by black people and in many black people a reluctance not to hate. It is always the experience of social change that groups whose conditions improve cannot in their feelings and behavior reflect the present but have to use their newly gained freedom and power to even the scores of the past. This will require, on the aggregate as well as on the individual level, helping methodologies designed to liberate people from the grip of development-disturbing historical loyalties which disable them, adaptively and productively, to deal with the social conditions and interpersonal relationship opportunities of the present.

In a similar vein women now are free to express the anger which many have felt and have had to suppress over long periods of time. Dramatically, as the anger becomes less and less justified, the more it has to be expressed, as if it were a mandate from the past that has now to be fulfilled. This makes the current wish for instant relationship even more difficult to achieve than the quest for immediacy would, in and by itself, suggest. Angry people are not likely to find or maintain loving partners. Recourse to lesbianism with its own conflicts and involvements will occur and produce new client groups for which past experiences may not fully provide guidelines of intervention.

In summary, it may be necessary to shift in many instances from a therapeutic orientation which was concerned with the dynamics of inhibited love to one which is concerned with the dynamics of uninhibited hate.

In more general terms and embracing all the points made in this book, professional helpers in medicine, law and social work will have to become more and more concerned with the increasing feeling of insignificance which Helen Harris Perlman has conceptualized as the "diminished man."[1] In a civilization of high complexity, the feeling of insignificance becomes everybody's actual or latent problem. The helper's task then must be performed in a general orientation of enhancing a patient's or client's dignity and potential.

REFERENCES

1. Helen Harris Perlman, "Casework and 'the diminished man'," *Social Casework,* Vol. 51, No. 4, April, 1970, pp. 216-224.

SUBJECT
INDEX

AUTHOR INDEX

LEADERSHIP OF DISCUSSION GROUPS
Case Material and Theory

By **Gertrude K. Pollak,** *Philadelphia, Pennsylvania*

This book examines the "group" as a therapeutic tool. It is concerned with the problem of reaching and holding groups and the tools for success in solving that problem. It contains records of actual group discussions with the author's commentary. Emphasis is placed on the techniques used in quiding group discussions, as well as the theory underlying this guidance. The book deals with group leadership techniques, discusses how to acquire and develop these techniques, and presents ways of teaching them to potential leaders.

CONTENTS: Development of a Family Life Education Program; Purpose and Scope of the Family Life Education Program; Outreach and Mobilization of Groups; Group Goals and Group Composition; Setting and Tools; The Physical Side of Sex Relations; Problems of Dating and Impulse Control of Retarded Teen-Age Girls; Talking about Love and Marriage with Unmarried Mothers; Discussing Sex and Drugs with Inner-City Boys; Answering Children's Questions about Sex; Reaching to and Handling of Children's Stealing; Problems of Overprotection and of Social Relations of Physically Handicapped Children; Coping with Sexual Needs after Divorce or Death of Spouse; Realistic and Unrealistic Expectations of Adult Sons and Daughters; Enriching One's Life in Retirement; The Discussion Content; How to Prepare It for and How to Handle it with Different Groups; Use and Control of Interpersonal Dynamics in the Relationships of the Leader to Group Members and of the Group Members to Each Other; Evaluation of Past and Planning of Future Group Discussions; Staff Development; The Training of Group Discussion Leaders.

ISBN 0-470-69175-1   1975

BASIC PSYCHOPATHOLOGY: A Programmed Text

Edited by **C.W. Johnson, J.R. Snibbe,** *and* **L.A. Evans,** *All of the University of Southern California School of Medicine*

The purpose of this book is to enable students of psychopathology to acquire skills in the systematic observation of patient behavior and data collection, the effective use of the Mental Status Examination, the correct application of psychiatric terminology to patients, and the recognition and classification of all commonly encountered psychopathologic syndromes. It is a patient centered, clinically oriented text. It is self instructional and programmed and is planned to incorporate educational principles which facilitate learning and make optimum use of the reader's time, and can be used as a primary text or as a supplement to another.

CONTENTS: Human Growth and Development (Infancy and Childhood); Human growth and Development (Adolescence, The Early and Middle Adult Years, The Later Adult Years); Mental Status Examination; The Organic Brain Syndrome; Functional Psychoses; Neuroses; Personality Disorders; Psychophysiologic Disorder; Transient Situational Disturbances; Depression; Suicide; Drug and Alcohol Abuse; Schizophrenia and Manic-Depressive Illness; Psychopathology in Childhood; Psychopathology in Adolescence; Mental Retardation

ISBN 0-470-44608-0   1975

SPECTRUM PUBLICATIONS, INC.
86-19 Sancho Street
Holliswood, New York 11423

Distributed solely by Halsted Press
Division of John Wiley & Sons, Inc.
605 Third Avenue, New York, N.Y. 10016

Please forward all orders to Halsted Press.

ISBN 0-470-15041-6